OUR
MAGNIFICENT
BASTARD TONGUE

OUR
MAGNIFICENT
BASTARD TONGUE

THE UNTOLD HISTORY OF ENGLISH

John McWhorter

GOTHAM BOOKS

GOTHAM BOOKS
Published by Penguin Group (USA) Inc.
375 Hudson Street, New York, New York 10014, U.S.A. •
Penguin Group (Canada), 90 Eglinton Avenue East, Suite 700, Toronto,
Ontario M4P 2Y3, Canada (a division of Pearson Penguin Canada Inc.) • Penguin Books
Ltd, 80 Strand, London WC2R 0RL, England • Penguin Ireland, 25 St Stephen's Green,
Dublin 2, Ireland (a division of Penguin Books Ltd) • Penguin Group (Australia),
250 Camberwell Road, Camberwell, Victoria 3124, Australia (a division of Pearson
Australia Group Pty Ltd) • Penguin Books India Pvt Ltd, 11 Community Centre, Panchsheel
Park, New Delhi - 110 017, India • Penguin Group (NZ), 67 Apollo Drive, Rosedale, North
Shore 0632, New Zealand (a division of Pearson New Zealand Ltd) • Penguin Books
(South Africa) (Pty) Ltd, 24 Sturdee Avenue, Rosebank, Johannesburg 2196, South Africa

Penguin Books Ltd, Registered Offices: 80 Strand, London WC2R 0RL, England

Published by Gotham Books, a member of Penguin Group (USA) Inc.

First printing, November 2008
3   5   7   9   10   8   6   4

Copyright © 2008 by John McWhorter
All rights reserved

Gotham Books and the skyscraper logo are trademarks of
Penguin Group (USA) Inc.

LIBRARY OF CONGRESS CATALOGING-IN-PUBLICATION DATA
McWhorter, John H.
Our magnificent bastard tongue: the untold history of English / John McWhorter.
      p.   cm.
Includes bibliographical references.
ISBN 978-1-592-40395-0
1. English language—History.   2. English language—Etymology.   3. English language—
Foreign elements.   4. English language—Foreign words and phrases.
5. Languages in contact.   I. Title.
PE1075.M597 2008
420.9—dc22   2008020983

Printed in the United States of America

Set in ITC Giovanni • Designed by Elke Sigal

While the author has made every effort to provide accurate telephone numbers and In-
ternet addresses at the time of publication, neither the publisher nor the author assumes
any responsibility for errors, or for changes that occur after publication. Further, the publisher does not have any control over and does not assume any responsibility for author or
third-party Web sites or their content.

Contents

Introduction

Was it really all just about words?

The Grand Old History of the English Language, I mean. The way it is traditionally told, the pathway from Old English to Modern English has been a matter of taking on a great big bunch of words. Oh, yeah: and shedding a bunch along the way.

You may well know the saga already. Germanic tribes called Angles, Saxons, and Jutes invade Britain in the fifth century. They bring along their Anglo-Saxon language, which we call Old English.

Then come the words. English gets new ones in three main rounds.

Round One is when Danish and Norwegian Vikings start invading in 787. They speak Old Norse, a close relative of Old English, and sprinkle around their versions of words we already have, so that today we have both *skirts* and *shirts*, *dikes* and *ditches*. Plus lots of other words, like *happy* and *their* and *get*.

Round Two: more words from the Norman French after William (i.e., Guillaume) the Conqueror takes over "Englaland" in 1066. For the next three centuries, French is the language of government, the arts, and learning. Voilà, scads of new words, like *army*, *apparel*, and *logic*.

Then Round Three: Latin. When England falls into the Hundred Years' War with France, English becomes the ruling language once more, and English writers start grabbing up Latin terms from classical authors—*abrogate* and so on.

Too, there are some Dutch words here and there (*cookie*, *plug*), and a little passel from Arabic (*alcohol*, *algebra*). Plus today we have some from Spanish, Japanese, etc. But those usually refer to objects and concepts directly from the countries in question—*taco*, *sushi*—and so it's not precisely a surprise that we use the native words.

These lexical invasions did leave some cute wrinkles here and there. Because when French ruled the roost, it was the language of formality; in modern English, words from French are often formal versions of English ones considered lowly. We *commence* because of French; in a more mundane mood we just *start*, using an original English word. *Pork*, *très* culinary, is the French word; *pig*—

très beastly—is the English one. And then even cuter are the triplets, where the low-down word is English, the really ritzy one is Latin, and the French one hovers somewhere in between: Anglo-Saxon *ask* is humble; French-derived *question* is more buttoned up; Latinate *interrogate* is downright starchy.

But there's only so much of that sort of thing. Overall the Grand Old History is supposed to be interesting by virtue of the sheer volume of words English has taken on. We are to feel that it is a good, and perhaps somehow awesome, thing that English has been "open" to so many words.

Yet even that doesn't hold up as well as often implied. Throughout the world, languages have been exchanging words rampantly forever. Languages, as it were, like sex. Some languages resist it to an extent for certain periods of time depending on historical circumstances, but no language is immune. Over half of Japanese words are from Chinese, and never mind how eagerly the language now inhales English words. Almost half of Urdu's words are Persian and Arabic. Albanian is about 60 percent Greek, Latin, Romanian, Turkish, Serbian, and Macedonian, and yet it is not celebrated for being markedly "open" to new words. Rather, quite simply, Albanians have had a lot of close interaction with people speaking other languages, unsurprisingly their vocabulary reflects it, and no one bats an eye. The same has been true with English—and Persian, Turkish, Vietnamese, practically every Aboriginal language in Australia, and . . . well, you get the point.

As such, the lesson that the difference between Old English and Modern English is a whole lot of new words is, for me, something of a thin gruel.

Don't get me wrong—words are nice. I like them. I am no more immune than the next person to taking pleasure in tasty etymologies such as that the word *tea* started way off in one dialect of Chinese, was taken up by Malays, and subsequently by the Dutch traders in their lands as *thee*, and was first pronounced "tay," coming to be pronounced "tee" only later, while that same *ea* spelling is still pronounced "ay" in names like *Reagan*.

Yet my impatience with the word fetish of typical popular treatments of The History of English is based in the fact that I happen to be a linguist. Etymology is, in fact, but one tiny corner of what modern linguistic science involves, and linguists are not formally trained in it. Any of us sought for public comment are familiar with the public's understandable expectation that to be a linguist is to carry thousands of etymologies in one's head, when in fact, on any given question as to where a word comes from, we usually have to go searching in a dictionary like anyone else.

Linguists are more interested in how the words are put together, and how the way they are put together now is different from how they were put together in the past, and why. That is, we are interested in what the layman often knows as "syntax," which we call grammar.

By grammar, we do not mean the grim little rules so familiar to everyone from school—i.e., "grammar school." We mean, for example, the conjugational endings on verbs in European languages (Spanish *hablo, hablas, habla*). We mean things like, in Japanese, word order is completely different from English, such that a sentence like *Craig met his wife in London* would come out *Craig London in his wife met*.

Think of it this way: you could cram your head full of every Russian word, and yet find that Russian six-year-olds were little Churchills compared to you walking around bursting with isolated words but unable to conjugate, mark nouns for case, use words in the proper order, or pull off any number of things fundamental to saying even the simplest things.

A Russian once told me sagely that it's better to be alone than to consort with just any person who happens into one's life: *Lučše byt' odnomu čem s kem popal*, which comes out literally as "Better to be alone than with who falls (i.e., "falls into one's orbit," "happens into the picture"). Uttering that meant that she knew to use a particular form of the word for *better* rather than another one, to use a particular case form on the word for *one* to mean "alone" (*odnomu*), and to mark the word for *who* in the instrumental case (*kem*) which, in that word, comes out irregular. She knew to use a particular form of the word for *fall* that one uses when referring to a single occurrence of falling (the *-pal* part of *popal*) rather than to the extended process of falling (in which case it would be a different form, *-padaet*).

Words alone, then, were only the very beginning of what she did in uttering that sentence, and really, to linguists not even the fun part. The fun part was how she combined the words to make a sentence. She was not only uttering Russian words one by one—she was subjecting them to grammar.

Well, English has grammar, too. Thus my frustration with The History of English as a story about words comes from the fact that The History of English is also a story about grammar. To wit, the pathway from *Beowulf* to *The Economist* has involved as much transformation in grammar as in words, more so, in fact, than in any of English's close relatives. English is more peculiar among its relatives, and even the world's languages as a whole, in what has happened to its grammar than in what has happened to its vocabulary.

As such, the focus on words cannot help but bring to

mind someone who has fitted out their ranch house with a second floor, knocked out all of the nonsustaining walls, and added on a big new wing on both sides, and yet month after month, all any of their friends mention when they come over is two new throw rugs.

One might object that the typical Grand Old History is not quite as negligent of grammar, in the linguist's sense, as I am implying. To be sure, popular treatments will often give it to the reader in bits and pieces.

Regularly, for instance, the layman will learn that whereas Old English was a language with ample conjugational endings and markers for gender and case, like Latin, over time it lost almost all of these. So, *man* was *guma*, but *The woman saw a man* was *Cwēn geseah guman*, because *-n* was an object ending. (The word *cwēn* comes down to us as *queen*, by the way.) Old English also split its nouns between masculine, feminine, and neuter: *the man* was *se guma*, but *the woman* was *sēo cwēn*.

Or we learn that the use of the *-ing* progressive form to mark the present tense—*You are reading this Introduction*—is something that started to creep into the language in the Middle English period. In Old English, I would much more likely have put it as *You read this Introduction*, just as one does in other European languages.

Okay, so we learn that English lost a bit of this and gained a bit of that. But this misses a larger picture. What is missing is that, compared to how languages typically change over time, English lost a perplexingly *vast* amount of grammar. Moreover, the grammar that it took on, like the *-ing* usage, seems ordinary only because we speak English. If we pull the camera back, the things English took on seem strikingly peculiar compared to anything its relatives like German and Swedish were then taking on— or in a case or two, what any languages on earth were taking on!

Modern English grammar is, in a word, weird.

English is one of about a dozen languages that are all so basically similar in terms of words and grammar, and mostly spoken so close to one another, that they all obviously began as a single language (although English is very much a prodigal son). The languages besides English include German, Dutch, Yiddish, Swedish, Norwegian, Danish, and Icelandic, plus some less familiar languages, like Faroese and Frisian, and Afrikaans in South Africa, which stemmed from the transplantation of Dutch amid the colonization of that country.

The parent to all of these languages was spoken about twenty-five hundred years ago in what is now Denmark (and a ways southward) and on the southerly ends of Sweden and Norway. We will never know what the people who spoke the language called it, but linguists call it Proto-Germanic. One might ask how we can even know that there was a language to give that name to. The answer is that we can reconstruct a great many of that language's words by comparing the words in today's Germanic languages and tracing back.

For example, English *daughter* is *Tochter* in German, *dochter* in Dutch, *datter* in Norwegian, *dotter* in Swedish, *dottir* in Icelandic. With techniques developed by linguists in the nineteenth century and refined since, we can deduce—with the help of now extinct Germanic languages preserved in ancient documents, like Gothic, in which the word was *daúhtar*—that all of these words are the spawn of a single original one, *daukhtrô*.

In all of the Germanic languages but English, their descent from that same ancient language is clear first, it is true, from their words. No Germanic language's vocabulary happens to be as mixed as English's, and so the others' vocabularies match up with one another more than English's does with any of them. German's word for *entrance* is *Eingang*, Dutch has *ingang*, Swedish *ingång*, Yiddish *areingang*, Icelandic *innganga*. Before the Invasion of the Words, Old English had *ingang*, but later, English took *entrance* from French.

However, the other Germanic languages are also variations on a single pattern in terms of how their grammar works. One can tell immediately, linguist or not, that they all began as one thing, like Darwin's finches. For a Dutch person, learning Swedish is no picnic because learning a new language is always hard, but there are few surprises. Nothing comes off as maddeningly counterintuitive (as, say, nouns being boys and girls in so many languages seems to English speakers). The Germanic languages other than English are about as similar as French, Spanish, Italian, and Portuguese.

English, however, is another story.

To see that English is the oddball, take a look at a sentence in English and German, where all of the English sentence's words happen to be good old native ones, having come down from Old English. No Old Norse, French, or Latin:

Did she say to my daughter that my father has come alone and is feeling better?

Sagte sie meiner Tochter, dass mein Vater allein gekommen ist und sich besser fühlt?

The words, you see, are not a problem. Even if you have never taken German, you can match up the German words pretty well with the English ones. *Sagte* is *said*, *Tochter* is *daughter, allein* is *alone,* and so on.

> *Sagte sie meiner Tochter,*
> said she to-my daughter

> *dass mein Vater allein gekommen ist*
> that my   father alone come   is

> *und sich   besser fühlt?*
> and himself better feels

Word for word, the German sentence is "Said she to my daughter that my father alone come is and himself better feels?" The way German puts the words together is a whole new world for an English speaker. English has *Did she say . . . ?* German has *Said she . . . ?* Why does English have that business with *Did she say . . . ?* Why *did*? "Did" what?

English has *to my daughter;* German bundles the "to-ness" onto the end of the word for *my, meiner*—i.e., German is a language with lots of case marking, like Latin. In English, case marking remains only in shards, such as the possessive *'s* and moribund oddities like *whom*. In English, one *has come*, but in German one *is come* (just as many will recall from French's grand old *passé composé: je suis venu*). Then, German has its business of putting verbs last in subordinate clauses: *alone come* instead of *come alone*, *better feels* instead of *feels better*.

And even more: in German's *sich fühlt* for *feels*, the *sich*, the only word that does not have an English equivalent, means "himself"—in German you "feel yourself" better, you "remember yourself" rather than just remembering, and in general, you mark actions having to do with feeling and thinking as done "to yourself." Finally, where German has *fühlt* ("feels"), English has *feel*-ing. How come German can use just the simple form *feels*, while we have to mark it with *-ing*?

Every one of these things is an obstacle to the English speaker's mastery of German. They all seem, to us, to come out of nowhere, just like the fact that German nouns come in masculine, feminine, and neuter flavors (*meiner* in *meiner Tochter* is the *feminine* dative; if a son were in question, then it would be *meinem Sohn*). Mark Twain, in his essay "The Awful German Language," nicely summed up the experience of an Anglophone learner of German: "The inventor of the language seems to have taken pleasure in complicating it in every way that he could think of."

The crucial fact is that an English speaker might be moved to make a similar assessment of all of the other Germanic languages, for pretty much the same reasons.

For example, the Dutch version of the sentence is *Zei zij tegen mijn dochter dat mijn vader alleen gekomen is en zich beter voelt?* in which the words occur in the same order as in the German.

The question is why, indeed, *Said she to my daughter that my father alone come is and himself better feels?* is so silly in English alone. The Germanic languages, of course, have their differences, and not all of them parallel the German one quite as closely as Dutch does. To a Norwegian, for instance, a sentence with the words in the German order of *Said she to my daughter that my father alone come is and himself better feels?* would seem a little off, but still highly familiar. The Norwegian version is:

Sa   hun til dattera   mi
said she to daughter my

at   faren   min er kommet alene
that father my is come   alone

og   føler sig   bedre?
and feels himself better

Here we have many of the same sorts of things that motivated Twain to say, "A person who has not studied German can form no idea of what a perplexing language it is." The same *Said she . . . ?* (*Sa hun . . . ?*), *is come* (*er kommet*), and "feeling yourself" (*føler sig*), plus gender: the *my* for *my daughter* is *mi* but the *my* for *my father* is *min.*

That is, in a sense one "should" be able to say in English *Said she to my daughter that my father alone come is and himself better feels?* After all, you can say something similar in every other offshoot of Proto-Germanic but English. Only to English speakers does the sentence sound like something someone with brain damage would say. This shows that something was different about how Old English evolved.

English's Germanic relatives are like assorted varieties of deer—antelopes, springboks, kudu, and so on—antlered, fleet-footed, big-brown-eyed variations on a theme. English is some dolphin swooping around underwater, all but hairless, echolocating and holding its breath. Dolphins are mammals like deer: they give birth to live young and are warm-blooded. But clearly the dolphin has strayed from the basic mammalian game plan to an extent that no deer has.

Of course, dolphins are also different from deer in being blue or gray rather than brown. But that is the mere surface of the difference, just as English's foreign words are just the surface of its difference from German and the gang. English is different in its whole structural blueprint.

This is not an accident. There are reasons for it, which get lost in chronicles of English's history that are grounded primarily in lists of words, words, words.

In this book, I want to fill in a chapter of The History of English that has not been presented to the lay public, partly because it is a chapter even scholars of English's development have rarely engaged at length.

Why is English grammar so much less complicated than German's—or Norwegian's, Icelandic's, or any other Germanic language's? Because the Scandinavian Vikings did more than leave us with words like *skirt* and *get*. They also beat up the English language in the same way that we beat up foreign languages in classrooms—and twelve hundred years later we are still speaking their close-but-no-cigar rendition of Old English!

Why does English use *do* in questions like, say, *Why does English use* do *in questions*? The reader is vanishingly unlikely to have ever encountered another language where *do* is used the way it is in English, and that's because linguists barely have either, out of six thousand languages in the world. Or is it just an accident that English speakers have to say *He is feeling better* where almost all the other Germanic languages would say *He feels better*—as would most languages in the world? Well, Welsh and Cornish, spoken in Britain long before English, and spoken alongside it for more than fifteen hundred years, have both the *do* and the *-ing* usages. Most scholars of The

History of English insist that this is just a coincidence. I will show that it is not. While the Vikings were mangling English, Welsh and Cornish people were seasoning it. Their rendition of English mixed their native grammars with English grammar, and the result was a hybrid tongue. We speak it today.

I want to share this first because it makes The History of English more interesting than successive waves of words, decorated with sidebars as to how the grammar changed a bit here and there for no particular reason. Second, once we know the real history of English, we can understand that certain things we have been taught about our language and how we use it are hoaxes. It is not true that saying *Billy and me went to the store* or *Tell each student that they can hand in their exam on Tuesday* is "illogical." Nor is it true that the structure of people's native language reflects, in any way we would find interesting, how they think. We will also see further counterevidence to the idea that English is uniquely "open" to new words, in little-known secrets about English's vocabulary before it was even considered English.

It's not, then, all about words that just happened into our vocabulary. It's also about things speakers of other languages *did* to English *grammar*, and actions speak louder than words. The real story of English is about what happened when Old English was battered by Vikings and bastardized by Celts. The real story of English shows us how English is *genuinely* weird—miscegenated, abbreviated. *Interesting.*

Let's go back to the middle of the fifth century A.D. in Britain, after the Romans left, and look a little more closely at the landscape than we are usually taught to.

OUR
MAGNIFICENT
BASTARD TONGUE

One

WE SPEAK A
MISCEGENATED GRAMMAR

THE WELSHNESS OF ENGLISH

The first chapter in the new history of English is that bastardization I mentioned.

German, Dutch, Swedish, and the gang are, by and large, variations on what happened to Proto-Germanic as it morphed along over three thousand years. They are ordinary rolls of the dice. English, however, is kinky. It has a predilection for dressing up like Welsh on lonely nights.

The Kinks

Did you ever notice that when you learn a foreign language, one of the first things you have to unlearn as an English speaker is the way we use *do* in questions and in negative statements? Take *Did you ever notice . . .* ? for example. Or *I did not notice*. We're used to this *do* business, of course. But it's kind of strange if you think about it. In this usage, *do* has no meaning whatsoever. It's just there, but you have to use it. One cannot, speaking English, walk around saying things like *Noticed you ever?* or *I not notice*. English has something we will call *meaningless do*.

Most languages, unsurprisingly, have no interest in using the word *do* in a meaningless way. If you've studied Spanish, you quickly learned that to put a verb in the past, you do not stick in a past form of the verb for *do*. *Did she talk?* is not **Hago** *ella hablar?* Nor do you jam in *do* to make a sentence negative—*She does not talk* is not *Ella no* **hace** *hablar* but *Ella no habla*. Nor is it *Elle ne* **fait** *parler* in French, or *Ona ne* **delaet** *govorit'* in Russian, *Hi lo* **osa** *ledaber* in Hebrew, or—you get the picture.

Did she walk? feels utterly conventional to us, when if you step beyond English, you look for *do* used that way and come up short.[1] None of the other Germanic languages use *do* the way English, ever the wayward one, does.

Then there is this *-ing* thing. We are given a tacit sense that tense marking in English works like this:

present:	I write
past:	I wrote
future:	I will write

1. To those who are up on their colloquial German and feel that Germans are no stranger to *meaningless do*, we'll get to that in a little while. Preview: Germans are, indeed, strangers to *meaningless do*.

But if you think about it, *I write* is not really present tense. Imagine you're at your laptop writing an e-mail and someone asks what you're doing and you say "I write." It's impossible to imagine that said by anyone without a foreign accent, and one imagines that the e-mail such a person would write would be full of mistakes. "I write" would be, quite simply, incorrect. Your answer would be "I'm writing."

"I write," on the other hand, is what you would say to express something more specific: that it's something you do on a regular basis. *I write, usually, from about ten A.M. to one P.M.* The present tense, in English, is expressed not with a bare verb, but with the progressive *-ing*. The bare verb has a different meaning, which linguists call *habitual*.[2]

Yet once again, that's not the way it is in any other language you learn. In Spanish, your answer if asked what you were doing would be *"Escribo."* The French person would answer *"J'écris."* Sure, both of these languages and many, many others have ways of calling attention to the

---

2. Actually, you might notice that there are indeed verbs where you don't use the progressive to speak of the present: *I know the truth* (you don't say *I am knowing the truth*), *I love dinosaurs, I have a scanner.* The issue here is that these types of verbs fall into a class linguists call *stative*: knowing, loving, and having are ongoing conditions, not actions—one does not say "I shall hereby perform the action of right now *having* this pencil!"; rather, having is something that just *"bes"* in an ongoing fashion. As such, these verbs are inherently *habitual*, and habitual verbs in English are bare.

fact that you are *in the process of writing the letter at this very instant*: in Spanish, *Estoy escribiendo*, in French, *Je suis en train d'écrire*. Germanic languages do, too, like German's *Ich bin am schreiben*, which comes out as "I am on the writing." But it's the decidedly peculiar individual who is given to stressing for every one of their actions that they are indeed *in the process of accomplishing it at this very instant*. In a normal language, you use a progressive construction when there's a reason to. Otherwise, to answer "I write" sounds perfectly fine in most languages. But in English, it sounds vaguely funereal, and *-ing* is the ordinary way to use the present tense.

English, then, is the only Germanic language out of the dozen in which there could be a sentence like *Did you see what he is doing*? rather than *Saw you what he does*? Since none of the other offshoots of Proto-Germanic seems to have sprouted oddities like these, one might ask whether there is a reason that English has.

And if one asks that, presumably it will strike one as germane that there happen to be languages with precisely the same oddities spoken right on the same island where English arose, long before English got there.

Yet most scholars of English's history find this neither germane nor, really, even interesting. Why?

Uninteresting Likenesses

The languages in question belong to another Indo-European subfamily, Celtic. There are only a few of these languages today, although they once held sway across vast swatches of Western Europe. Irish Gaelic is one of them (and its variant Scottish Gaelic, an export to Britain, another). But the ones most of interest to us are those of Britain: Welsh in Wales and Cornish in Cornwall.[3] The last native speaker of Cornish died in 1891, but there is a hardy revival movement for it today.

If English is the odd one out as Germanic languages go, Celtic languages are odd ones out as Indo-European languages go. Verbs sometimes coming last in German strikes us as weird enough, although it is actually ordinary worldwide. But in Celtic, verbs come *first* in a sentence, which is less ordinary worldwide, and downright freaky within Indo-European languages. There are other features in which Celtic marches to the beat of its own drum, and two of them are the way it uses *do* and *-ing*.

Take a look at this in Welsh. *Nes* means "did." Welsh puts words in a different order than English, and so *nes* is always first. What's interesting is that it is there, just as in English:

---

3. There was also an indigenous people in present-day Scotland called Picts. Most likely they spoke a Celtic language, too, but we have no evidence to be sure of this.

Did I open?	*Nes i agor?*
I did *not* open.	*Nes i* ddim *agor.*
I opened.	*Nes i agor.*

Welsh uses *do* in the same meaningless way that English does. *Do* just sits there taking up space, not contributing any meaning to the sentence.

Note that Welsh is different from English in one way: it uses *do* in "normal" sentences, affirmative ones as well, as we see in that third sentence. When a Welshman states *Nes i agor*, they are using the words that come out in English as "I did open," but not with an emphatic meaning as in our *I **did** open*. They mean it as if we were speaking English in the Elizabethan period and said, "Since it was so hot out, I did open a window for you."

But in that people still said things like that then, English was more like Welsh than it is today. Even further back in Middle English, one might say for "You wept" *Thou **dudest** wepe*. Our sense that to speak fake "Olde English" means sticking "dosts" and "doths" all over the place corresponds to a Middle English reality, which persisted for centuries afterward. Here is Gertrude in *Hamlet*, addressing same:

Alas, how is't with you
That you *do* bend your eye on vacancy,

And with th'incorporal air *do* hold discourse? (III, iv, 120–22)

Upon which he answers (147–48):

My pulse as yours *doth* temperately keep time,
And makes as healthful music.

English has gone its own way since and dropped this *do* usage in affirmative ("neutral") sentences, keeping it in the negative and question contexts. But there was a time when English was even more like Welsh on this score than it is now.

Or how about English's progressive construction, as in *Mary is singing*. In English, *-ing* leads a double life. In one guise, it makes a verb into a gerund, which means that it makes the verb into a noun. One sings, and one may enjoy that which is known as *singing*, a noun: *Singing is fun*. As a matter of fact, gerunds are sometimes called "verb-nouns."

Then, *-ing* has a second identity, when it is used in the progressive construction: *Mary is singing*. Here, *singing* is not a verb-noun—*Mary is singing* does not mean "Mary embodies the act of rendering song." *Singing* in *Mary is* *singing* is just a verb, specifically what is called the present participle form of a verb. Our *-ing* is two things.

The important point is the fact that in English, as we have seen, this progressive *Mary is singing* construction is our present tense. If someone asks you what you're doing as you warble "Just the Way You Are," your answer must be "I'm singing," not "I sing." Interestingly, in Welsh as well, to answer that question you must use a progressive construction: Welsh and other Celtic languages have the same *-ing* fetish as English. Remembering that Celtic word order is odd to our eyes and ears, in Welsh, if someone asks, "What's our Mary doing?", the answer is not "Mary sings" but "Mary is in singing":

Mae Mair yn canu.

is   Mary in singing

Canu is the verb-noun for *sing* in Welsh: "Mary is in the act of singing."

Now, to be sure, in Welsh the present is expressed with a verb-noun progressive, while in English's *Mary is singing* progressive, *singing* is not a verb-noun but a participle. However, the participle is just a latter-day morphing of what *started* as a verb-noun. Just as with meaningless *do*, what English does now is a drifting from what first was even more like Celtic.

It went like this. In Old English one could say "I am on hunting" to mean that you were hunting. This was, obviously, just like the Welsh "Mary is in singing." Then in Middle English, the *on* started wearing down and one might say "I am a-hunting," just as we now say "Let's go" instead of "Let us go."

Then before long, the *a-* was gone completely—as in the way we casually say "'Tsgo" for "Let's go"—and hence, just "I am hunting." Ladies and gentlemen, the birth of a present participle. Celtic was English's deistic God—it set things spinning and then left them to develop on their own. But that first spin—*I am on hunting*—was key. It was just like Welsh.

And it's not just Welsh. Cornish down south has the same kinks about *do* and *-ing*. The way to say *I love* is:

Mi a wra cara.
I   at do love

Sort of an Elvisesque "I'm a-doing loving," except it is a perfectly normal sentence in Cornish, and its *do* is used the same way with negative sentences and in questions:

Gwra   cara?
do-you love

Then it has the same mysterious drive to use verb-nouns for the present tense. Here is *She is buying vegetables*, in which the word for *buy* is a verb-noun:

Yma hi **ow prena** *hy losow.*
is   she at   buying her vegetables

So: the Angles, Saxons, and Jutes brought a language to Britain in which a sentence like *Did you see what he is doing*? would have sounded absurd. The people already living in Britain spoke some of the very, very few languages in the world—and possibly the only ones—where that sentence would sound perfectly normal. After a while, that kind of sentence was being used in English as well.

And yet specialists in the history of English sincerely believe that English started using *do* and *-ing* by itself, and that it is irrelevant, or virtually so, that Welsh and Cornish have the same features. You can page through countless books and articles on The History of English, and even on specifically the history of meaningless *do* or the *-ing* present, and find Celtic either not mentioned at all, actively dismissed, or, at best, mentioned in passing as "a possible influence" (read: of no significant bearing upon the issue).

There is clearly something strange about this, but it is not that legions of scholars are incompetent, stubborn, bigoted against Celts, or anything else of the sort. Rather, they come at the issue with certain established assumptions, reasonable in themselves, which if held, understandably leave one comfortable treating such close correspondences between English and Celtic as accidents.

Those assumptions, however, are mistaken.

Assumption Number One:
The Celts All Just Died

The first assumption is that after their arrival in England in A.D. 449, the Germanic invaders routed the Celts in more or less a genocide, leaving mere remnants huddling on the southwesterly fringes of the island. From here, it has traditionally been concluded that Celtic languages could not have had any impact on English for the simple reason that no Celtic speakers survived the genocide to influence the language.

But the truth is that the genocide of an entire society inhabiting vast expanses of territory is possible only with modern technology. The Angles, Saxons, and Jutes did not possess anything we would consider modern technology. How, precisely, were they to kill practically every Celt outside of Wales and Cornwall—that is, in an area about the size of New England? With swords? How many people can you get at? Remember, there weren't even guns yet. And even when Dutch and English colonists in South

Africa had guns, African peoples there, like the Xhosa and the Zulu, gave them enough of a run for their money with spears that even though the whites ended up subjugating the blacks under apartheid policies, the blacks still today vastly outnumber the whites. There was no way to kill everybody.

In that light, whatever havoc the Germanic invaders wrought, there were not, apparently, very many of them. Early Anglo-Saxon chroniclers like the Venerable Bede had it that the invaders "overran" Britain. But writers of their era did not have access to substantial and regular news from all over the land, satellite photography, or our conceptions of demography or even scholarship. Bede was even writing three centuries after said "overrunning," which as Bill Bryson notes "is rather like us writing a history of Elizabethan England based on hearsay." Bede could easily document as "overrunning" what was actually a compact number of violent, destructive encounters.

Comparative genetics has recently confirmed that this was the case. By tracing mutations in mitochondrial DNA in women and on the Y chromosome in men, we can reconstruct the migrations of human populations since the emergence of *Homo sapiens*. It turns out that only about 4 percent of British men's genetic material is traceable to a migration from across the North Sea. Moreover, essentially none of British women's genetic material traces back to such a migration, meaning that the invaders were not couples with children, such that women and young'uns would bulk up the total. Rather, the invaders were just a bunch of guys. In fact, evidently the famous Germanic invaders numbered about 250,000, about as many people as live in a modest-sized burg like Jersey City.

We will never be able to bring the Celts of this era back to life to ask them whether they felt terribly "exterminated," nor do official records survive that would allow us to check for ourselves. However, there have always been clues that are problematic for the genocide account. A burial site with graves both in the style of Germanics across the North Sea and in the style of Celts (with the body buried crouching and facing north or northeast) suggests not genocide, but Celts living alongside Germanics. The very fact that after the invasion, archaeologists find no abrupt transformation in material culture suggests that Celts survived in numbers robust enough to pass on their cultural traditions permanently.

A valuable snapshot comes in the laws established by Ine, a seventh-century king of Wessex (in an era before any individual considered himself the king of England as a whole). Two centuries after the Angles and company supposedly exterminated the Celts, the stipulations of Ine's laws indicate a Britain where Celts are numerous and well integrated into society. The *wealhs* (*Welshmen* in modern parlance) Ine repeatedly refers to and legislates for include lowly slaves, respectable landowners, and even horsemen serving the king. The main lesson, as Ine devotes one law after another to establishing precisely how much compensation a Welshman's family or owner gets if he is killed, is that subjugated though they usually were, the Celts were *there*, in numbers.

The scenario Ine's laws depict brings to mind, in fact, the situation of American blacks before Emancipation, right down to the fact that *wealh*, while coming down to us as *Welsh*, was not the name the people had for themselves (which was *Cymry*), and in Old English meant "foreigner," with a goodly tacit implication as well of "slave." In southern America before the end of the Civil War, Africans and their descendants were subjugated, but were still part of the warp and woof of existence for whites, outnumbered them, and included in their number a class of free farmers and artisans.

The genocide story, then, has fallen apart. Genes, archaeology, documentary evidence, and sheer common sense leave it dead in the water. Typical assumptions such as magisterial popular chronicler David Crystal's that the Celts hung around for a brief spell as slaves and brides but their "identity would after a few generations have been lost within Anglo-Saxon society" can no longer be accepted.

This leaves us with a simple fact about what happens when languages come together: they mix. There is no recorded case in human history in which languages were spoken side by side and did not spice one another with not only words, but grammar. This means that even without recordings of seventh-century Celts speaking "Englisc" and peppering it with phrasings copying Celtic grammar, we can assume that this was the case, because it quite simply must have been.

Taking a cue from the slavery analogy, we see that Jamaicans today speak a hybrid language, popularly called patois, that was born when African slaves learned English and filtered it through the languages they had been born to. Here is a sentence in patois:

Unu main mi tingz, no tiek non gi im.
You all mind my things, don't give him any.

The word *unu* is unfamiliar in English itself, but it is the word for *you* in the plural in the Igbo language of Nigeria, which many early slaves in Jamaica had grown up speaking. Patois phrases it *Don't take any give him* because many West African languages string verbs together in just this way, such as the Twi language also spoken by many African slaves in Jamaica:

> *O   de   sekan   no   ma   me.*
> he took knife   the gave me
> "He gave me the knife."

The patois case is an example of what happens when there are so many people speaking a language in a non-native way that new generations speak it that way instead of the original way.

There are similar cases around the world. Another one involves the famous click sounds in a family of languages, Khoisan, spoken in southern Africa by hunter-gatherers. Those clicks are extremely rare worldwide. Outside of the southern half of Africa, the only language in the entire world with clicks is a way of talking, now extinct, that speakers of one tiny aboriginal Australian language made up for use in male initiation rites! (The people's everyday language is Lardil; the click talk was called Damin.) Among the languages with clicks in southern Africa, as it happens, are several that are not in the Khoisan family but are spoken nearby, such as Zulu and Xhosa (the native language of Nelson Mandela). Given that clicks essentially do not exist anywhere else, it is obvious that earlier forms of Zulu and Xhosa mixed with click languages.

The way that English uses *do* and *-ing* just like Celtic, then, is predictable. Celts, less exterminated than grievously inconvenienced, had to learn the language of the new rulers. The Celts' English was full of mistakes—that is, ways of putting words together that worked in Celtic but were new to Old English. However, over time, this Celtic-inflected English was so common—after all, there had only ever been 250,000 Germanic invaders—that even Anglo kids and Saxon kids started learning it from the cradle. After a while, this *was* Englisc—just as in Jamaica, after a while, *Don't take none give him* was the way one spoke English there, and in what is now South Africa, using click sounds like the hunter-gatherers became the way one spoke Xhosa.

Right? Well, for History of English scholars, still not. The genocide is, to them, only one reason to see the Celtic-English mirrorings as accidental.

Assumption Number Two:
Shitte Happens

The body of scholarship on The History of English is replete with detailed descriptions of meaningless *do* and the verb-noun present tense just "happening." We are to assume that chance alone could have nudged English into coming up with meaningless *do* and a verb-noun present.

To the scholars working in this vein, meaningless *do*

and the verb-noun present are just same-old same-old as languages go. To them, saying that English got these features from Celtic just because Celtic has them is like proposing that anteaters, because they have long tongues and eat insects, must have evolved from chameleons. In that case, we easily see that plenty of animals have long tongues and even more eat bugs, such that there is no scientific reason to assume that anteaters evolved from chameleons.

The problem is that these scholars have usually had little occasion to look hard at languages outside of the Germanic family. They are unaware that, as it were, in actuality very few languages have long tongues, and that even fewer both have long tongues and also eat bugs. They do not realize how very special English is—or that it is inescapable that Celtic languages made it that way.

In the *do* case, the distraction is that in many colloquial dialects of Germanic languages, one can use *do* in a way kind of like English's meaningless *do*. But only kind of.

The issue is sentences like this colloquial German one:

Er tut   das schreiben.
he does that write

This means "He writes that," and in terms of word order, it certainly looks like Ye Olde *do* in the *Hamlet* passages—that is, it looks like German's version of *He doth write*. However, in fact, it isn't—it is something quite different.

For one, German's version is optional. One might say *Er tut das schreiben*, but the simple *Er schreibt das* is also alive and well, and in fact, much more usual.

Then, most importantly, meaningless *do* is meaningless, but German's *do* is meaningful. It is used when you want to emphasize some part of the sentence. When you put stress on what you want to emphasize, you might also toss in a *do*. So: imagine if now and then you fall into moods where you enjoy taking a knife and stabbing pillows open. Suppose you run out of pillows but you still have that nagging urge, and then you see a laundry bag bulging full of clothes. A thought balloon pops up over your head: *Maybe I'll cut the **bag** open!*

Well, in German the thought balloon would read:

*Ich **tue** vielleicht den Sack *aufschneiden*.*
I   do maybe the bag cut-open

So, German *do* is an optional trick, used only in the present tense, as one factor in the way you emphasize something. Obviously this is nothing like the way we use *do* in English, in which to negate a sentence or to make it a question, you have to stick in a *do* no matter what, and the *do* has no meaning of its own. No dialect in any Germanic language other than English uses *do* in this way; at best, there are dialects that use it in variations on how German does.

History of English specialists seem to suppose that it's just that English merely drifted one step beyond German's *do*—making it required instead of optional. But if that were so natural, so same-old same-old, then surely it would have happened in some other Germanic language sometime. Also keep in mind that each Germanic language comes in a bunch of dialects, many of which are quite different from the standard. If meaningless *do* is so unremarkable and could have "just happened," then surely some small dialect of something somewhere— some villagers in the northern reaches of Sweden, some farmers down in some Dutch dell, some Yiddish speakers in a shtetl—somebody, *somewhere* would have come up with their own meaningless *do* just by virtue of shitte happening. But they haven't.

Nor *do*, apparently, any other human beings beyond Europe. Meaningless *do* is not a long tongue—it's a tongue used as a leg. Some readers will think perhaps of a language like Japanese, where quite often a verbal concept is expressed as "doing" a noun, such as *travel* being rendered as *to do travel*; here is *Taroo travels*:

Taroo ga ryokoo o suru.
Taroo   travel   does

Persian is like this, too, so much that it has only a few hundred verbs per se—to speak Persian is to be accustomed to "doing a waking up" instead of awakening someone, and so on. But in both of these cases, *do* has literal meaning: one is "doing," performing, the noun. And in neither language is *do* used with *all* nouns as meaningless *do* is used with all verbs. Japanese and Persian's *do* is a meaningful word; meaningless *do* is a little cog of grammar that happens to have the shape of the actual word *do*.

I make no claim to have checked all six thousand languages in the world for a meaningless *do*, but I am aware of precisely two approximations of it anywhere but in Great Britain, and then, only approximations.

One is in a small language called Nanai spoken in Siberia, where it is *be* rather than *do* that is used meaninglessly. To say *They died*, you can say "They died was."

Hjoanči buikiči bičin.
they   died   was

This does not mean "They were dead" or "They were dying": the *was* is the third-person singular form, not the third-person plural form that would agree with *they*. The *was* word is just tacked on, with no meaning: "They died—uh, was." A more graceful translation would be something like "What it was is that they died." But even this is optional, like the Germanic *do*s.

Then there is the Monnese dialect of Italian and a few other close relations, out of dozens of Italian dialects, where the word for *do* is used in questions:

Ngo   fa-l   ndà?
where do-he go
"Where is he going?"

But in these Italian varieties, *do* is not used in negative sentences, whereas in English, *do* is used in both negative and question sentences—just as in Welsh and Cornish. And then, in Welsh and Cornish, *do* is also used in "default" affirmative sentences and was as well in earlier English—Gertrude in *Hamlet*'s "That you **do** bend your eye on vacancy." So, in some Italophone *hamlets*, so to speak, *do* has been yoked into service in a meaningless fashion—but not in the particular way that it was in English, which mirrored precisely how *do* was used in the Celtic languages spoken by the people whom Anglo-Saxon speakers joined in invading Britain.

The only languages in the world that are known at present to have meaningless *do* as English does are (drumroll, please) none other than the Celtic languages. Can we really believe that the Celts had nothing to do with English's meaningless *do*, which parallels it so closely *and once did so even more*? In fact, do we have any reason to consider that the Celts were anything less than the crucial factor, without whom English would have no meaningless *do*?

This question looms ominously over all of the specialists' "shitte happens" versions of how English got meaningless *do*. All of them are brilliant in themselves, but also seem to ignore that meaningless *do* as it exists in English is about as weird as finding an AMC Gremlin on the moon.

One specialist tries that it all started with *do* being used to indicate that something is done on a regular basis—*Cats do eat fish* would mean "Cats are in the habit of eating fish"—and that something odd happened in negative versions of sentences like that. At first, *Cats do not eat fish* meant "Cats are in the habit of not eating fish," as a kind of description of something specific about cat's gustatory disinclinations. It was a description of a habit of cats, with *do* as the habitual marker. But obviously that sounds like a rather labored way of saying "Cats don't eat fish," and that's exactly how people started processing it. Instead of "What cats do is not eat fish," people heard "Cats eating fish is a 'no.'" That is, they heard the negation as the most prominent feature in the sentence and thought of the "habit" part as background. Thus a sentence that was first about *do*-ness became one about *not*-ness. *Do* started to seem like just some bit of stuff hanging around. It lost its "juice" and stopped meaning "regularly," and eventually meant nothing at all, functionless like a hallowed old politician given a sinecure in acknowledgment of services rendered back in the day. Voilà, meaningless *do*.

Now, if you didn't quite get that or had to read it again in order to do so, it's not surprising. To be sure, it follows more gracefully when expressed in terminology that academic linguists are trained in, and the article in question is one of the most elegantly written pieces of scholarship I have ever read; it has always been, to me, almost pleasure reading—I'd take it to the beach. Yet the explanation is still a distinctly queer, Rube Goldberg turn of events. Nothing like that is documented to have happened to the word *do* in any other language on earth, and besides, the author even admits that in almost half of the sentences in the Early Middle English documents he refers to, *do* does not, in fact, indicate that something happens regularly.

"Future research" will figure out why, he has it—but how about if future research shows that what created meaningless *do* was not that English speakers for some reason drifted into the peculiar hairsplitting reinterpretation of *Cats are not in the habit of eating fish* as meaning

"It is not that cats eat fish," but the fact that the people who lived in Britain long before English got there had meaningless *do* already?

Then there are those who claim that meaningless *do* was a natural development in response to various ways that English's grammar changed from Old to Middle English. For example, in Old English, verbs could sit in various places in a sentence—at the end, at the beginning, and so on, depending on what was next to it. In Middle English and beyond, verbs started sitting in the middle, after the subject and before the object, the way they do now (*The boy kicked the ball*). But there was an intermediate point when the general pull was toward the verb's being in the middle, but there were still sentences like *Wherefore lighteth me the sonne?* ("Why does the sun light me?") where the verb *lighteth* is before the subject *sun*. One way of thinking has it that meaningless *do* came in because when you use it, the verb ends up in the middle the way sentences by Middle English were supposed to go:

Wherefore lighteth me   the sonne?
            verb   object subject (Oh, no no!)

Why does the sun light me?
              subject verb object (*That's* the ticket!)

Yeah—but the question is where English even got a meaningless *do* to use in this way. In languages all over the world since the dawn of human speech, at first the verb can hang around at the ends or beginnings of sentences and then at some point the verb is restricted to sitting in the middle; it happens all the time. And nowhere—nowhere—else on earth have such languages taken the word *do* and turned it into a meaningless little helper in order to nudge this along.

Biblical Hebrew put verbs first; Modern Hebrew puts them in the middle. Yet no one in Israel today is using the Hebrew verb for *do* in a meaningless way. The Arabic of the Koran puts the verb first; it has since morphed into the vast array of today's actual spoken Arabics, stretching from Morocco across northern Africa into the Middle East, as well as down into Nigeria, Chad, and Sudan. Not one—*not one*—of these modern Arabic dialects has a meaningless *do*.

So, where oh where might English have gotten that meaningless *do* in order to whip its verbs into line? According to the History of English folks, in trying to figure that out, we are to ignore that the languages already spoken in Britain . . . I don't even need to finish the sentence. It may well be that corralling verbs into the middle of the sentence made a meaningless *do* useful. But only English had a meaningless *do* available in the first place—as used by Welsh and Cornish speakers. Welsh and

Cornish, then, were together the reason English has a meaningless *do* today.

English's verb-noun present also looks, to traditional specialists, as if it is just one step past something in other Germanic languages. Again, there is a big picture they are missing.

Now, the sheer presence in a language of a progressive construction using a verb-noun is not all that extraordinary. It happens here and there that people say that they are "in" an action to say that they are *in the process of accomplishing it at this very instant.* This includes the Germanic languages. In German you can say, as I mentioned before, *Ich bin am schreiben* for "I am writing." Similarly, in Dutch it would be "I am on the writing," *Ik ben aan het schrijven,* and Norwegian has something similar with *Jeg er åt å skrive.*

English is peculiar, however, in taking the ball and running with it, to the point that the bare verb is nosed out completely. That is something much rarer in languages, popping up only in obscure corners here and there. Basque is one, a language related to no other one on earth. Or there is one little dialect of Greek (Tsakonian, for the record) that has booted bare verbs in the present and uses a progressive, for no reason anyone can see.

But then, another of the obscure corners in question is good old Celtic. English is the only Germanic language that developed in a context where Celts were the original inhabitants—and English is also the only Germanic language that turned its verb-noun progressive into its only present tense.

However, History of English specialists adhere to a just-so story in which the verb-noun present "just happened" by itself. Old English had two progressive constructions. One was the verb-noun one, *I was on hunting*, but another one used a participle form of the verb, marked with *-ende*. "I was following" was *Ic wæs fylgende*.

Now, today we do not say "I was huntende." To the experts, *I was hunting* rather than *I was on hunting* happened because for some reason speakers started having a hard time telling *-ende* and *-ing* apart and settled on using *-ing* in the *-ende* construction.

But that *-ende* was an inheritance from Proto-Germanic. As such, other Germanic languages have their versions of *-ende* today, and no one confuses them with anything. German's *-ende*, for instance, is doing just fine. Once in Germany I told a waitress not to put onions in my salad or I would become *der kotzende Fremder* ("the vomiting foreigner"). In earlier German, just as in earlier English, there was an *-ende* progressive; here is an Old High German sentence:

Ist er ouh   fon   jugendi filu   fastenti.
is he indeed from youth   much fasting
"From his youth on he has been fasting much."

But then meanwhile, German drips with *-en* suffixes
on both nouns and verbs, including their version of *I was
on hunting, Ich bin am schreibe*n ("I am writing"). Yet in a
thousand years, this *-en* suffix has not been "confused"
with *-ende*. Was it really just a shrug of the shoulders that
supposedly led English speakers to confuse their *-ende*
with *-ing*, which is much less similar to *-ende* than is German's *-en*? Nowhere else in the Germanic family is the
-ende ending so prone to "collapsing" into other ones.
Why was *-ende* so uniquely subject to the vapors in only
English? Historians of English are producing a description
based on what they see in the documents over time rather
than explaining it.

And the traditional version is hopeless in explaining
why the verb-noun progressive, once established when
-ende was "confused" with *-ing*, metastasized and became
the verb-noun *present*, i.e., the only way to express the
present short of sounding like a Martian by answering
"I write" when someone asks what you're doing. Why
couldn't *I am hunting* have stayed as meaning "I am *in the
process of hunting at this very instant*"? That is, as it has in all
of the other Germanic languages? Scholars charting the

triumph of the verb-noun progressive over the bare verb diligently note how the progressive becomes ever more common—14 percent progressive! 45 percent! 67 percent! 92 percent!!!!!—rather than wondering why nothing remotely similar ever happened to any of the other languages that Proto-Germanic morphed into. They are describing, but not explaining.

The Celtic account, then, is more useful in the sheer scientific sense than the old one. It provides an answer to what specialists have been shrugging their shoulders about for eons: just why the verb-noun (*-ing*) ejected the participle (*-ende*) and just why the progressive became the only way to express the present tense. Welsh and Cornish express their progressive with a verb-noun and not with a participle. Welsh and Cornish use their progressive instead of bare verbs in the present tense. Period.

Yet among the specialists, to propose that the English progressive construction is a copy of Celtic's is considered a renegade point. Certain wobbly speculations continue to be reproduced in sources both scholarly and popular. Maybe, we learn, Anglo-French scribes were hazy on the difference between *-ende* and *-ing*—which leaves unexplained how scribal errors on codexes read in candlelight by a tiny literate elite would have affected the way millions of mostly illiterate people out on the land spoke.

The likeness between English and Celtic is so close in

this case that the only thing that would seem to save a traditionalist approach is the old assumption that there were barely any Celts around. And as we have seen, that assumption can't stand.

So:

1. The Angles, Saxons, and Jutes encountered Celtic speakers.
2. Meaningless *do* in the affirmative, negative, and internegative is found nowhere on earth except in Celtic and English.
3. English is the only Germanic language that uses its verb-noun progressive as the only way to express present tense; Welsh and Cornish do the same.

Asked what those three facts signify as to why English has meaningless *do* and and verb-noun present, all human beings would draw the same conclusion—except those who know more about the history of the English language than anyone else in the world. What could the blockage possibly be?

Assumption Number Three:
Writing Is How People Talked

It's a timing issue. On its face, the specialists seem to have a point, especially with meaningless *do*. Old English speakers met Celts starting in A.D. 449. This would be when Celts started learning and transforming the English language. Yet there is not a hint of meaningless *do* in any English document until the 1300s, in Middle English. Century after century of Old English writings and no meaningless *do* at all. Why does it show up so late?

The verb-noun progressive pops up in Old English now and then, in sentences like *Ic wæs on huntunge* for "I was hunting." But today other Germanic languages also have their "on hunting" constructions when they want to stress "progressiveness," and so on its face this does not make Old English look at all strange as its family goes. And in any case, more often, the progressive is the *-ende* one as in *Ic wæs fylgende* for ("I was following.") In fact it is the *-ende* progressive that becomes a little more common in later Old English.

So Old English does not look terribly Celtic, and to traditional scholars this proves that the Celts cannot have been the source of meaningless *do* or the verb-noun present. What historians of English see is that English with meaningless *do* and a verb-noun present ruling the roost does not show up in documents until past the halfway point of English's entire documented life span. If Celts mashed their mix-ins into English, then why did they take almost a thousand years to do it?

But that question proceeds upon a fundamental mis-

conception about what ancient written evidence tells
us—or doesn't—about how the language was spoken
every day.

Writing and talking are very different things. This is
clear to us when it plays out in our own times with our
own languages: in the entire eighty-five-year run of *Time*
one could miss that in casual speech people say "whole
nother." But when we are dealing with languages of an-
tiquity, whose casual renditions we cannot experience,
the gulf between writing and speaking cannot help but be
less apparent. We will never know how Old English was
spoken by illiterate farmers; the written version that survives for us to peruse is the only rendition of the language
we will ever know. However, people way back when were
no more given to gliding around talking like books than
we are, and in fact, writing and talking were much more
different for them than for us.

In ancient times, few societies had achieved wide-
spread literacy. Writing was primarily for high literary, li-
turgical, and commercial purposes. Spoken language
changed always, but the written form rested unchanging
on the page. There was not felt to be a need to keep the
written form in step with the way people were changing
the language with each generation.

For one, each language was actually spoken as a group
of dialects very different from one another, such that there

was no single spoken variety to keep up with. As long as the written form was relatively accessible to the general population, however they actually spoke, then the job was done. Old English, for example, came in four flavors: Northumbrian, Mercian, Kentish, and West Saxon. Most Old English documents are in the West Saxon dialect, because Wessex happened to become politically dominant early on. But this means that what we know as Old English is mostly in what is properly one dialect of Old English, and the speakers of the other dialects just had to suck it up. They did, and there is no evidence that anyone much minded.

In addition, there was always a natural tendency, which lives on today, to view the written language as the "legitimate" or "true" version, with the spoken forms of the language as degraded or, at best, quaint—certainly not something you would take the trouble of etching onto the page for posterity with quill and ink. As such, the sense we moderns have that language on the page is supposed to more or less reflect the way the language is spoken would have seemed peculiar to a person living a thousand years ago, or even five hundred.

In Europe, for example, it was the technology of the printing press and the democratic impulses in the wake of the Reformation that led to calls for written material in local languages. Until then, people in France, Spain, Italy, and Portugal readily accepted Latin—a different language entirely from what was spoken "in the street"—on the page. Similarly, for many centuries, Slavic language speakers were used to ancient Old Church Slavonic as a written lingua franca, although no one spoke it. Sanskrit was long the written language par excellence in an India where its offshoots, such as Hindi, had long since emerged and thrived as spoken languages.

Until well into the twentieth century, for Indonesians, the written language of books and newspapers and the one taught in school was Classical Malay, about as different from how people actually spoke as Shakespeare's English is from how we do. Even today, although standard Indonesian is more in step with everyday speech than Classical Malay, it is still not the way anyone would actually converse casually who wanted to date or have friends. Indonesians giggle to see the spoken rendition of their language put on a blackboard, just as English speakers would find it inappropriate to see *Time* written in the dialect of rappers.

Among people worldwide before five hundred years ago, this kind of gulf between written and spoken language was, in a word, a norm. In the late 1200s, Dante considered himself to be venturing a special gesture in writing *La Vita Nuova* in Italian instead of Latin, only doing so because he wanted the work to be accessible to a woman who did not know much Latin. In Dante's world, Italian as we know it had long existed as an everyday language—Dante himself spoke it 24/7—but the ordinary thing was to write in Latin. Latin was what Italian (and French, Spanish, and the other Romance languages) had been a thousand years before. But since Latin hit the page first—Latin "called it!" as kids say in grabbing a seat—a millennium later, there still reigned a sense that Latin was fit for the page, while Italian was just "the vulgar tongue," as even Dante put it, "in which even housewives can converse."

There is a similar situation today in Arabic-speaking countries. In, say, Morocco, the Arabic used in writing is one thing, preserved on the page and kept as close to the language of the Koran as possible. The Arabic actually spoken is another thing, morphed fifteen hundred years away from the written variety and now a different language entirely. A Moroccan will recall learning "Arabic" in school, so different is the standard variety from the "Arabic" they learned at home.

Moreover, in each Arab nation, the standard has drifted into a spoken dialect in different ways such that the spoken Arabic in each place is a different language from the others. So, *good* in the standard is *jayyad*, but look at what it is in different countries in the Arab world:

Saudi	*zeen*
Iraqi	*xoos*
Syrian	*mniiḥ*
Lebanese	*mliiḥ*
Egyptian	*kuwayyis*
Algerian	*amliiḥ*
Tunisian	*baahi*
Libyan	*ṭayyeb*
Moroccan	*mezyan*

To Arabic speakers, the preservation of Standard Arabic on the page, and only occasionally or even never seeing the language they actually speak in print, feels normal. It is even seen as an advantage in forging ties between different Arab nations.

It is in this light that we return to the fact that the Celtic impact shows up in English documents only long after the Celts and the Old English speakers had first come into contact. The personnel in question did not live in anything like our world. They lived lives in which there were no potatoes, tomatoes, coffee, tea, chocolate, spinach, broccoli, or sugar. They didn't need last names because most of them spent their lives in small villages where everybody knew one another. Dismemberment and murder were so common that adjudicating their outcomes was the main focus of suites of laws penned by kings like His Highness Mr. Ine.

And, by and large, speakers of Old English did not read. Writing was better described as *scripture*—a formal, ritualized, elite pursuit, preserved via scribes copying old texts century after century, sequestered in thick-walled edifices from the hurly-burly of actual everyday speech. In this rigidly classist world, casual English—especially the kind associated with *wealhs*, who were usually slaves—was no more likely to wind up engraved in ink than the charming babblings of toddlers.

As such, the only reason that Celtified English started coming through in writing even in the 1300s was a historical accident.

The year 1100 is when, largely, Old English stopped and Middle English, an almost curiously different thing, began. Middle English was, indeed, a profound transformation of Old English. Partly, yes, in terms of words—a bunch of French ones started pouring in—but also in terms of grammar. When the Norman French conquered England in 1066 and established French as the written language of the land, for the next century-and-a-half there is almost no written English that has survived. Then after relations with France began to sour in the early 1200s and English started to be used as a written language again, we see a brand-new, slimmed-down English, as if it were in an "after" picture in a diet ad.

Old English had been jangling with case markers, and nouns had three genders as in Latin, Greek, and Russian.

In Middle English, waking up like Rip Van Winkle around 1200, case and gender were largely as they are now: vestigial and absent, respectively.

In Old English, words like this one for *stone, stān,* took different suffixes according to case and number. Suddenly in Middle English, the only case suffix left is genitive (possessive), and the plural one is the same in all cases. Suddenly, in Middle English we are, in other words, home.

	Old English	*Middle English*
the stone	stān	stone
the stone's	stānes	stone's
to the stone	stāne	to the stone
the stones	stānas	the stones
the stones'	stāna	the stones'
to the stones	stānum	to the stones

The question, though, is whether this all really happened in 150 years, and certainly it did not. Languages do not suddenly chuck away their case markers, almost as if people speaking languages with lots of them find them, deep down, as burdensome as we Modern English speakers do when exposed to them in classrooms in Latin and Russian. Greek, like Russian, has been chugging along for millennia with enough case markers to sink a ship.

Sure, languages will slough off a suffix here and a suffix there, just like we do our eyelashes. Just as sure, some languages will slough off more suffixes than others, just as many men go bald on their heads but retain hair, well, elsewhere. But even that takes time. No language "goes bald" in just a century-and-a-half.

Rather, in languages' documentation we watch these things happen *gradually*—century by century, as with those few more hairs you keep spotting on the shower drain as the years pass. Old High German had a Latin-style fecundity of case and gender inflection. Modern German has much less (although still a lot by English standards). We can watch that happening in a majestic procession of documentation over almost a thousand years—not just 150, roughly the time since the end of the Civil War! And even then, the end result was not a language as denuded of case and gender as English, but the German that so frustrated Mark Twain.

For this reason, on the stark difference between the English of *Beowulf* and the English of *The Canterbury Tales*, even specialists agree that there is some discrepancy between what we see in the documents and what was the living reality of everyday Old English. Namely, Middle English is what had been gradually happening to *spoken* Old English for centuries before it showed up in the written record.

The Old English in writing, then, is the language as it

was when the Germanic invaders brought it across the North Sea, preserved as a formal language, a standard code required on the page, kept largely unchanging by generation after generation of scribes and writers imitating the language of the last. The language used every day was quite different, not policed and preserved the way the written language was, free to change naturally as all spoken language does, such as by losing suffixes one by one.

The only thing that led writers to start actually putting this "real" Old English on the page was the 150-year blackout period. When people started writing English once more, the written Old English standard could not exert the pull that it once had. These were now documents of another time. One hundred and fifty years was a vaster amount of time to a Dark Ages Englishman than it is to us—he had no photos or newspapers as we do of the Civil War, and no audio recordings as we do of the 1890s onward—and the continuity between generations of scribes preserving the old language had been broken. It was as the French had taken over Dante's Italy for 150 years, imposing French as the language of writing. Imagine if after the French left, writers were no longer competent in Latin and felt more comfortable writing in the language people actually spoke, Italian.

In this light, our timing problem with the Celtic features is solved.

Traditional specialists understand that Old English

was losing its case markers gradually even though writers wrote as if this wasn't happening. As such, they should be able to accept that "Celty" English would also have been spoken out on the ground even though no one would have deigned to transcribe it amid the formality of the written word. This is not a studied argument designed to get around something about Old English, but a call to bring scholarship on The History of English in line with the realities of how different writing was from casual speech in the ancient, semiliterate world.

We can assume that Celts were speaking Celtified English starting with the first generation who grew up bilingual, as far back as the fifth century, and throughout the Old English period. However, this was not the English from across the North Sea—Celtified English was likely thought of as "mixed" or at least funny-sounding English for a long time. As such, it would never have been committed to print—and in a world without audio recording technology, this means that this kind of English as spoken during the entire reign of Old English is hopelessly lost to us.

However, starting in the Middle English period, when it became acceptable to write English more like it was actually spoken, this would have included not only virtually case-free nouns, but also our Celticisms. Therefore, it is not that Celticisms only entered English almost a thousand years after Germanic speakers met Celts in Britain. It is merely that Celticisms did not reach the page until then, which is quite a different thing.

People writing the way they actually talked was quite rare anywhere in the world until rather recently, and even today it is by no means universal.

The truth, then, is that if meaningless *do* and the verb-noun present did pop up in the first Old English documents, or even in Old English documents at all beyond the occasional peep, it would be very, very strange. We would expect that the constructions would show up only after a historical catastrophe such as the Norman occupation, after which, in many ways, England learned to write again. If the Battle of Hastings had not put a 150-year kibosh on written English, then "real" English might not have been committed to print until as late as after the Reformation, in the 1500s.

In the obituary of someone who started some famous chain of stores, often the date that the first establishment opened seems much earlier than you would have expected. The first McDonald's, for example, opened in 1955. That doesn't "feel" right: McDonald's was an entrenched part of American life only ten years after that or more. For example, there is an *I Love Lucy* episode from 1956 where Lucy and Ethel are making a long road trip and running low on food, as fast-food restaurants alongside interstate highways were not yet ubiquitous. For a long time after 1955, McDonald's restaurants were in business, but because they had yet to proliferate widely, to most people they were barely known. The first Wendy's was opened in 1969—my intuition would have put it in about 1978.

Likewise, the Celtic imprint on English would have thrived below the radar long before it appeared regularly in print, even when meaningless *do* and the verb-noun present had long been well established as ordinary speech. They just weren't being publicized in commercials yet, so to speak. Since there was no recording technology, we can't hear Old English speakers using them. But they did. We know that because English was the only Germanic language spoken by people whose native languages had the selfsame traits.

One Last Assumption: Where Are the Celtic Words?

There is one last thing that misleads linguists into thinking the Celts could not have had any significant impact on English: the fact that there are, essentially, no words in English that trace to Celtic.

One might expect there to be some, after all. The Vikings left a whole mess of their words, as did the Normans. One would presume that when large numbers of people start using a language imposed on them and start speaking it in their own way, that they will sprinkle their version of the language with a lot of their own words. The Vikings left behind their *get* and *skirt* and even their *their*; the Normans left behind seemingly every word we use to step beyond humility. So where are the long lists of Welsh and Cornish words?

Instead, there are only a dozen-odd words that have been traditionally traced to Celtic, and most of them are arcane, obsolete ones introduced by Christian missionaries from Ireland. Naturally, then, experts assume that the Celts must have just learned English the way they encountered it and added nothing to it. This assumption is reasonable. It is also mistaken.

The fact is that people scattering their own words into their new language is not a universal. It might happen— the Vikings did it; the Slavonic-speaking people who picked up Latin in what is now Romania did it to Romanian. But it might not.

Russian, for example, has some quirky features that show that at some point way back, it was learned by so many speakers of another language that it was never the same again in terms of *grammar*. The culprit was a language of the family called Uralic. Its most famous members are Finnish and Hungarian, but other ones have long been spoken across a vast expanse of what is now northern Russia. In Russian, it seems odd that in negative sentences an object has to be rendered as "of" itself: "I see a girl" is *Ja vižu devočku*, but "I do not see a girl" is *Ja ne vižu devočki* where the *-i* ending connotes "of-ness" ("I do not see of a girl"). Odd, that is, until you notice that Finnish and its relatives do that same thing. In Russian, unlike in a "card-carrying" Indo-European language, you do not "have" something: rather, something "is to" you: "I have a book" is *U menja kniga* ("to me is a book"). Again, something similar is par for the course in Finnish.

No one interested in the Russian-Uralic encounter denies that Russian picked up these and other things from speakers of Finnish-related languages. It's as if your child comes back from summer camp with some downloaded music they never listened to before, from some friends they met who were into that kind of music.

Yet there are at very best about a couple of dozen Uralic words in Russian, most of them obscure. The Vikings left about a thousand in English, and the Normans left ten thousand. Yet the Uralic speakers left just a handful in Russian. We will never know just why; certainly it was due to specific cultural factors lost to us because the people had no writing.

It is the same in India: in the southern part, there is a smallish family of languages, Dravidian, completely unrelated to the other ones, which are of the Indo-Aryan subfamily of Indo-European. When you hear that a person from India speaks Tamil, for instance, that is a Dravidian language, as unlike Indo-Aryan Hindi, Bengali, Gujarati, and the others as Finnish is unlike English. In any case, along the barrier between the Dravidian area and the Indo-Aryan area, people have often been bilingual in Dravidian and Indo-Aryan languages—but over the past thousand years, almost no Dravidian words have seeped into Indo-Aryan languages. Yet Indo-Aryan words are fairly dripping with features in their grammars which, again, no linguist denies are the result of Dravidian speakers learning Indo-Aryan ones.

It also bears mentioning that, really, etymology is not the most rigorously policed of fields. Much of the basic work was done long ago under different standards of evidence than linguists would admit today; there are a great many holes ("etymology unknown"), and legions of etymologies that, if linguists were moved to seriously examine them today, would fall apart. In that light, there is some work suggesting that there are at least a few more Celtic words in Modern English than once thought. Candidates include *brag*, *brat*, *curse*, and *baby*.

In any case, the paucity of Celtic words in English is no argument at all against meaningless *do* and present-tense *-ing* being due to Celtic influence. It's interesting—the work that argued that Dravidian languages decisively shaped Indo-Aryan grammar is today cherished as sage, classic, and incontrovertible. Yet a very similar argument about Celtic and English is received as quirky, marginal, and eternally tentative.

Celtic Underground Even Today

To show how ordinary it would have been for a "Celtified" expression to almost never make it onto the page over centuries' time, here is a living example. There is a queer little wrinkle in regional dialects in the north of England. Standard English verb conjugation in the present tense involves one thing: tacking on *-s* in the third person singular:

I walk	we walk
you walk	you walk
Diana **walks**	Diana and Francesca walk

In the northern dialects in question, instead the rule is that you tack on the *-s* in all persons and numbers:

I walks	we walks
you walks	you walks
Hyacinth walks	Betty and Shirley walks

Except for one thing: in the third person plural, when you use the pronoun *they* instead of nouns like *Betty and Shirley*, or *children*, or *McDonald's outlets*, you drop the *-s*:

I walks	we walks
you walks	you walks
Hyacinth walks	they **walk**

So Betty and Shirley *walks*, but they *walk*.

Weird, isn't it? There is nothing like it in any Germanic language but English. But there is something just like it in—need I even finish the sentence?

With the Welsh verb, in the third person plural, when nouns like *Betty and Shirley* are involved, the conjugational ending is the same as for the third person singular one. Again, verbs are first, and so Welsh has *learned she* for *she learned*, *learned Betty and Shirley* for *Betty and Shirley learned*:

*dys**godd** hi* ("she learned")
*dys**godd** Betty a Shirley* ("Betty and Shirley learned")

But if you use the pronoun *they*, the verb takes a third person plural ending:

*Dys**gon** nhw* ("they learned")

Cornish has the same thing.

Thus in Welsh, Cornish, and these dialects of English, how you conjugate the verb in the third person plural varies according to whether the subject is a noun or a pronoun. In itself, that seems an arcane and, to anyone but a linguist, dull thing. But for our purposes, the crucial fact is that no Germanic language other than English knows anything like this.

And overall, in terms of English or any European language beyond Celt land, this quirk, which linguists call the Northern Subject Rule, is one of those "Who'd a' thunk it?" things. Even History of English specialists see it as an oddity: it is not a run-of-the-mill development that happens in this and that language randomly like, say, conjugational endings.

In fact, it is something that happens occasionally in one specific type of language: the roughly one in ten worldwide that *put the verb first*. Like Tagalog in the Philippines. Or like . . . hmm. Thus we can form a good idea as to why these English dialects have taken on such a bizarre trait.

Yet the reader, especially if American, is unlikely ever to have known of the Northern Subject Rule, because it happens to have taken hold only in northern British dialects. Standard English developed from dialects far southward, and so the Northern Subject Rule has remained a strictly spoken feature, uttered countless times daily and evaporating into the air, recorded on the page only by occasional diligent dialecticians. It is unassailably Celtic, and yet unknown in the pages of *The Economist*, and always will be.

Crucially, there is no reason that meaningless *do* and the verb-noun present could not have thrived in obscurity in the exact same way until "real" English got to come out of the closet in the 1200s. The Northern Subject Rule is living the same closeted life today, showing us clearly that what is written can often be strikingly different from what is said.

What Is Proof?

As to whether English has a goodly dose of Celtic in it, at this point there is little that The History of English orthodoxy has left to deny it.

The scholars working in the traditional vein seem unable to arouse genuine interest in changes in the language that they cannot trace step-by-step in the documents starting as soon as they emerged. Hence the judgment on the issue in a benchmark study of Middle English: "There might be something to say for Keller's and Miss Dal's assertions that the ancient Britons were not exterminated but became amalgamated with the Germanic invaders and assumed their language while retaining some syntactical peculiarities of their ancient native tongue, but such statements remain necessarily hypothetical for lack of documentary evidence."

Even though that was written in 1960 (hence the "Miss Dal"), mainstream sentiments have not changed since. Developments that cannot be followed from when they started are, to the experts, not worth extended engagement.

But following changes in English starting from when they hit the ground in casual speech is a luxury available only from documents dating from when English was written more or less as it was spoken. Old English was almost never written that way. The Celtic impact must be embraced in the frame of mind of, say, a paleontologist who reconstructs the behavior of dinosaurs from fragmentary but indicative clues.

There are pathways of footprints left by herds of sauropod dinosaurs, the Brontosaurus (okay, Apatosaurus) type, in which smaller footprints run in the middle while the bigger ones run along the sides. Paleontologists have inferred from this that younger sauropods were protected by being flanked by the big older ones, as among some animals today. We will never have film to prove this, and most likely will never resurrect sauropods with DNA and watch them do it. Yet it is accepted that the paleontologists' reconstruction is a valid approach to the evidence available, and almost certainly correct.

The likenesses between Celtic languages and English are a similar case. Realities of the history of writing among human beings in ancient semiliterate societies make it impossible that we would find meaningless *do* in Old English documents like *Beowulf*, the Lindisfarne Gospels,

Aelfric's Colloquy, or Cædmon's Hymn, even if meaningless *do* was being used casually every day all over
England. Yet the presence of the same feature in Welsh
and Cornish, and its absence used this way anywhere else
in the known world, make treating it as something that
just happened all by itself in English seem almost strange.

Overall, scholars of English's history are less resistant
to than uninterested in the impact of Celtic. The reason,
one senses, is that charting how Celtic languages shaped
English does not involve using the tool kit they are accustomed to. These scholars are trained to examine aspects
of English grammar that really did emerge by themselves
and were never thought of as "bad" or "peculiar," and
thus were committed to the page not long after they got
going.

Going is, in fact, a good example, in the *going to* future
marker, English's alternate to good old *will*. This is the
kind of thing English specialists love to sink their teeth
into. In Old English, there was no such thing as using the
word for *go* to put a verb in the future as in *I'm going to
think about that*. *Go* was about going somewhere and that
was that. Even as late as Shakespeare, at the end of the
1500s, *go* still meant *go*. In *Two Gentlemen of Verona*, the
Duke asks Valentine, "Sir Valentine, whither away so fast?"
and he answers, "Please it your Grace, there is a messenger
that stays to bear my letters to my friends, and I am *going*

to deliver them (III, I, 54–57)." Valentine means that he is literally going in order to deliver the letters.

However, if you are going in order to do something, then automatically what you are going in order to do will actually occur in the future. As such, Valentine's statement could be taken as meaning that his delivery of the letters will occur in the future—that is, that he *will* deliver the letters. Because of that ever-looming implication of futurity whenever one said *going to*, after a while *going to* started to actually mean the future rather than actual going.

It is about fifty years after *Two Gentlemen* that Charles I, amid the crisis that would soon cost him his head, rallied the gentry of Yorkshire saying, "You see that My Magazine is going to be taken from Me." (Poor Charles, for the record, was not complaining that he was to be deprived of his *Sports Illustrated*; by *magazine* he meant "arms depot," more pertinent to his situation.) This was a usage of *going to* that was not literal—the arms depot could go nowhere. *Going to* here had become a future marker like *will*, and wouldn't you know, around the same time in 1646, a grammarian popped in specifying that now "'going to' is the signe of the Participle of the future."

There is ample scholarly work on how *going to* went from referring to locomotion to becoming a future tense marker, complete with statistical analysis, tables, and so on. It's great stuff, and it's what a scholar of language change is trained in.

However, charting how Celtic languages impacted English involves different strategies. It requires being a different brand of linguist. Often, that brand is language contact specialist. That person has an eye on what sorts of features are common around the world and what sorts are not, is obsessed with not just one language family but with several, and has a native taste for history as well as linguistics. Such linguists are less tickled by things that sprung up in a language by themselves than by things that languages did to one another.

As such, it's as if scholars of The History of English are engaged in a lusty game of Monopoly when adherents of the Celtic idea bust into the room asking who wants to play a game of Clue. Or, some people are building things with an Erector set and someone pops in with a little car made of Legos. To the traditional specialist on how English got from *Beowulf* to *The Economist*, drawing parallels between English and some other language is just Not What They Do, especially not at any length. That feeling is understandable, but the problem is that the language contact specialist's analysis, in this case, squares with logic in a way that the same-old same-old analysis simply does not.

Frankly, another likely factor is that Irish, Welsh, and

Cornish are not languages anyone is apt to become familiar with who is not of Celtic ancestry. Andrew Dalby, working outside of the academy, has a way of getting such things tartly right. On the Celtic question, he gets in that "few English linguists know Welsh, so the similarities tend to be overlooked or played down." Yep—I highly suspect that if Welsh were, say, for some reason regularly taught in schools across Western Europe and in America, as French and Spanish are, then to linguists, raised with "schoolboy" Welsh, the parallels between Celtic and English would seem glaringly obvious and would long ago have been accepted as having a causal rather than correlative relationship.

However, here in real life, even to seasoned linguists, Celtic languages are, as often as not, remote oddities, bristling queerly on the page à la the likes of *Sut rydych chi?* meaning "How are you?" in Welsh. *Rydych???* How do you even pronounce that?? To someone whose foreign language competence is in French and German, there is nowhere to grab on to here. One moves on.

All that understood, the facts tell a story even if we will never have the "documentary evidence" of the kind the scholar quoted above was accustomed to working with. Swords and grimaces could not have exterminated a race of millions of Celts and left a few huddling in Wales and Cornwall. Rather, Celts, albeit subjugated, lived on throughout Britain in vast numbers. The Germanic invaders, like dominant classes worldwide at the time, enshrined a version of their language on the page that reflected what it was like before it came to be spoken and reshaped by the people who, albeit subjugated, continued to vastly outnumber them, and who passed their rendition of the language on to future generations both Germanic and Celtic. After the Norman French conquered the country, English was rarely written for a century-and-a-half, and when English was reawakened on the page thereafter, it suddenly had a grammatical flavoring that paralleled no languages on earth but Celtic ones, while English's relatives over on the Continent developed nothing similar.

Those facts lend themselves to an analogy about people we will call the Robinsons and the Joneses.

In 1870, Mr. Robinson and his family move to a small town in Illinois called Summerfield. Thirty years later, in 1900, the town's newspaper does a story about how Mr. and Mrs. Robinson and their three offspring have developed an unusual deftness in playing the piano with their feet. They play only with their feet, never with their hands, and can manage pleasant renditions of classical sonatas. The story also notes that the Robinsons' elderly next-door neighbors, the Joneses, have the same skill, as do their kids.

The news story does not tell us whether the Robinsons learned to play the piano with their feet from the Joneses. However, it does note that the Robinsons were close friends with the Joneses and that the Joneses' son Thaddeus even married the Robinsons' daughter Minerva.

Researching the issue in 2008, we find two other things. First, in 1880, researchers in the new field of sociology did an extensive study of the town the Robinsons moved to Summerfield from, Wistful Vista. And even in their chapter on the arts in Wistful Vista, which includes a detailed description of the town's musical scene, there is nary a mention of anyone playing the piano with their feet. Nor in the annals of descriptions of, or reports from, any other mid-nineteenth-century Illinois towns is there any record of people playing piano with their feet, just as today the practice is unheard-of in Ohio or anywhere else.

Second, Mr. Jones, having made his way into serving as Summerfield's water commissioner, left his papers to the local museum, and among them is a daguerreotype of him playing the piano with his feet way back in 1850, long before the Robinsons moved into the house next door.

Obviously, this evidence makes it rather plain that the Robinsons picked up their quirky approach to piano playing from the Joneses. However, imagine modern historians instead insisting that the Robinsons learned to play the piano with their feet on their own, despite that the Joneses right next door, their close friends, had been doing just that long before the Robinsons moved to Summerfield.

Our historians craft elaborate webs of motivation that would lead the Robinsons to take off their shoes and socks, hoist up their legs, and attempt "Chopsticks" with their toes. Mr. Robinson was a banker—maybe he developed repeat stress syndrome in his hands from using the telegraph machine while communicating with banks out of town and found that the only way he could play the piano was with his pedal digits. Maybe Thaddeus, whom the article described as a spirited fellow "full of the dickens," was as a tyke given to athletic stunts like putting his bare feet on the keyboard.

Yes, maybe. But all of this leaves the outside observer wondering what the use is of concocting scenarios like this. The scenarios would seem, ultimately, to be for some reason turning a blind eye to an obvious explanation. What purpose does it serve, we ask, to deny that the Joneses taught the Robinsons how to tickle the ivories with their feet? And what is the use of pointing out that the Robinsons don't *dress* much like the Joneses? (That's the part about Celtic words, in case the analogy is slipping!)

Or even: why conclude that the Joneses may have been

"just one influence" on the Robinsons? "Acknowledging" both sides is of no use in this case. The Robinsons learned how to play the piano with their feet from the Joneses. Period. If the Joneses had not already been playing the piano with their feet, the Robinsons would not be, either.

The judgment must be the same on Celtic's impact on English. The facts in this particular case do not lend themselves to mere parenthetical civil surmises that Welsh and Cornish "may have *influenced*" English grammar, with the treatment otherwise proceeding as usual, describing meaningless *do* and the verb-noun present drifting into existence by themselves for no reason. The facts do not indicate that the Welsh and Cornish features merely pitched in on a process that would have happened by itself anyway. If Old English had been brought to an uninhabited island—or, say, Cyprus, Greenland, or Fiji—rather than an island where Celtic languages were spoken, then there would be no such thing as a Modern English sentence like *Did you see what he's doing?* That sentence would be rendered as *See you what he does?*, as it is in any normal Germanic—or European—language.

English is not normal. It is a mixed language not only in its words, but in its grammar. Every time we say something like *Did you see what he's doing?*, we are structuring our utterance the way a Welsh or Cornish person would in their own native tongue. When well-intentioned chroniclers take in from scholarship on The History of English that "the English language has been indifferent to the Celts and their influence" (Robert McCrum, William Cran, and Robert MacNeil's *The Story of English*) or that "the Celtic language of Roman Britain influenced Old English hardly at all" (David Crystal's *The Cambridge Encyclopedia of the English Language*), they have been misled, despite the brilliance of their books overall (both of these are among my favorite books of all time).

English is not, then, solely an offshoot of Proto-Germanic that inhaled a whole bunch of foreign words. It is an offshoot of Proto-Germanic that traded *grammar* with offshoots of Proto-Celtic. The result was a structurally hybrid tongue, whose speakers today use Celtic-derived constructions almost every time they open their mouths for longer than a couple of seconds. *Do you want to leave now? What's he doing? Did he even know? What are you thinking? I don't care. She's talking to the manager.*

Celtic grammar is underneath all of those utterly ordinary utterances in Modern English. Our language is a magnificent bastard.

Two

A Lesson from the Celtic Impact

The "Grammatical Errors" Epidemic Is a Hoax

Oh, those *lapses*, darling. So many of us walk around letting fly with "errors." We could do better, but we're so slovenly, so rushed amid the hurly-burly of modern life, so imprinted by the "let it all hang out" ethos of the sixties, that we don't bother to observe the "rules" of "correct" grammar.

To a linguist, if I may share, these "rules" occupy the exact same place as the notion of astrology, alchemy, and medicine being based on the four humors. The "rules" make no logical sense in terms of the history of our language, or what languages around the world are like.

Nota bene: linguists savor articulateness in speech and fine composition in writing as much as anyone else. Our position is not—I repeat, *not*—that we should chuck standards of graceful composition. All of us are agreed that there is usefulness in a standard variety of a language, whose artful and effective usage requires tutelage. No argument there.

The argument is about what constitutes artful and effective usage. Quite a few notions that get around out there have nothing to do with grace or clarity, and are just based on misconceptions about how languages work.

Yet, in my experience, to try to get these things across to laymen often results in the person's verging on anger. There is a sense that these "rules" just must be right, and that linguists' purported expertise on language must be somehow flawed on this score. We are, it is said, permissive—perhaps along the lines of the notorious leftist tilt among academics, or maybe as an outgrowth of the roots of linguistics in anthropology, which teaches that all cultures are equal. In any case, we are wrong. Maybe we have a point here and there, but only that.

Linguists' Frustration

Over the years, some of the old notions have, in truth, slipped away, although this is due less to the suasive powers of linguists than to the fact that the particular rules in question were always so silly anyway.

No one taken seriously thinks it's wrong to end a sentence with a preposition anymore, such that *That's a store I wouldn't go to* is "awkward." Similarly, the grand old rule that one does not split infinitives is on the ropes. In our guts, few of us truly feel that there is anything wrong with where *slowly* is placed in *Imagine—to slowly realize that your language lost all of its suffixes as of this morning*!

The preposition rule was cooked up in the seventeenth century under the impression that because Latin doesn't end sentences in prepositions, English shouldn't. That makes one wonder when we are going to start cutting our English to conform to Arabic, Russian, Mandarin, and other languages with grand histories and literatures. The split-infinitive business was a nineteenth-century fetish, and may also have been based on the fact that Latin doesn't split infinitives—because its infinitives are just one word! We say *to end*; Latin had *terminare*, period, as unsplittable as the atom was once thought to be.

But the "rules" that have hung around make no more sense than those two, and yet laymen cling to them like Linus to his blanket.

Take the idea that it is wrong to say *If a student comes before I get there, they can slip their test under my office door*, because *student* is singular and *they* "is plural." Linguists traditionally observe that esteemed writers have been using *they* as a gender-neutral pronoun for almost a thousand years. As far back as the 1400s, in the *Sir Amadace* story, one finds the likes of *Iche mon in thayre degree* ("Each man in their degree").

Maybe when the sentence is as far back as Middle English, there is a sense that it is a different language on some level than what we speak—the archaic spelling alone cannot help but look vaguely maladroit, as if Middle English speakers were always a little tipsy on their mead.

But Shakespeare is not assumed to have been in his cups when he wrote in *The Comedy of Errors*, "There's not a man I meet but doth salute me / As I were **their** well-acquainted friend" (Act IV, Scene III). Later, Thackeray in *Vanity Fair* tosses off "A person can't help their birth."

Yet the notion that this usage is "wrong" holds on so hard that even linguists have to submit to their publishers' copy editors' insistence on expunging it, which answers the question we often get as to why we do not use constructions like this in our own writing if we are so okay with them. My own books are full of resorts to *he*, which I find sexist, occasional dutiful *she*s, which strike me as injecting a stray note of PC irrelevance into what I am discussing, or *he or she*, which I find clumsy and clinical—for the simple reason that I was required to knuckle under. At best I can wangle an exception and get in a singular *they* or *their* once or twice a book. (I must note that the copy editor for this book, upon reading this section, actually allowed me to use singular *they* throughout the book. Here's to *them* in awed gratitude!)

Or there's the objection to nouns being used as verbs. These days, *impact* comes in for especial condemnation: *The new rules are impacting the efficiency of the procedure.* People lustily express that they do not "like" this, endlessly writing in to language usage columnists about it. Or one does not "like" the use of *structure* as in *I structured the test to be as brief as possible.*

Well, okay—but that means you also don't "like" the use of *view, silence, worship, copy, outlaw,* and countless other words that started as nouns and are now also verbs. Nor do many people shudder at the use of *fax* as a verb.

The linguist notes that in a language with a goodly number of endings showing what part of speech a word is, making a noun into a verb means tacking the appropriate ending onto it. In French, the noun *copy* is *copie*; the verb "to copy" is *copier*. But in a language like English with relatively few endings, making a noun into a verb requires no extra equipment, and so *copy* becomes just *copy*. This is not a quirk of English—i.e., a loosey-goosey stipulation linguists make out of "permissiveness"—but typical of countless other languages in the world that don't make much use of suffixes to mark parts of speech. In Cantonese Chinese, *lengjái* can mean "good-looking guy," "to become good-looking," and "good-looking": noun, verb, and adjective. No one in China is writing in to newspapers complaining about it.

But somehow, a sense persists that nouns becoming verbs in English is icky, a messy transgression. Told that English speakers have been, as it were, turning *fax* into *fax* forever, people remain convinced that there's still something "wrong" with it. And we won't even get into how people feel about *Billy and me went to the store* and the idea that *me* is wrong because it's an object pronoun referring to a subject. (Actually, we will get into it, but not just yet.)

Trying to get into the head of how people feel about these things even when presented with linguists' protestations, I sense that the resistance is based on an understandable pride in having mastered these "rules." You've got your ducks in a row, and except when exhausted or on glass number three of wine, you have no trouble producing *Billy and I*. You learned what subjects and objects are, you learned your Parts of Speech. As such, you don't like someone coming along and deeming your effort and vigilance worthless. It must feel like someone telling you that it would be perfectly appropriate, natural even, to give in to the untutored impulse to chew with your mouth open.

The problem is that with all due understanding of that feeling, the "rules" we are taught to observe do not make sense, period. All attention paid to such things is like medievals hanging garlic in their doorways to ward off evil spirits. In an ideal world, the time English speakers devote to steeling themselves against, and complaining about, things like *Billy and me*, singular *they*, and *impact* as a verb would be better spent attending to genuine matters of graceful oral and written expression.

Over the years, I have gotten the feeling that there isn't much linguists can do to cut through this commitment to garlic-hanging among English speakers. There are always books out that try to put linguists' point across. Back in 1950, Robert Hall's *Leave Your Language Alone!* was all over the place, including a late edition kicking around in the house I grew up in. Steven Pinker's *The Language Instinct*, which includes a dazzling chapter on the grammar myths, has been one of the most popular books on language ever written. As I write, the flabbergastingly fecund David Crystal has just published another book in the tradition, *The Fight for English: How Language Pundits Ate, Shot, and Left*. But the air of frustration in Crystal's title points up how persistent the myths are. Maybe we just can't get through.

However, in this chapter I want to venture one more stab. If you understand that the phrasing of *Did you see what he's doing?* was injected into English by non-native speakers, and that there was once an English where no one would have put it that way, and that then, for a while there was an English where lots of people were putting it that way but it sounded quaint and awkward to others, you are in a position to truly "get" the message. The message: the notion that people are always "slipping up" in using their native English is fiction.

Now Versus Then

There is a paradox in how lovers of language often process English and the way it varies from mouth to mouth from decade to decade.

No one has trouble with the fact that the Old English of *Beowulf* is a different language than Modern English. On the contrary, the pathway from then until now is seen as a noble procession. First, majestic, flinty strophes of Old English handwritten on ancient paper, chronicling kings and battles and laws and such, a language closely akin to German. Then, Middle English: Chaucer, Sir Gawain, a language with a certain queer dignity on the page, not exactly what we speak but obviously related: *Whan that Aprille with hise shoures soote / The droghte of March hath perced to the roote.* Our tendency is to pronounce it with a vaguely Swedish lilt, which makes it pretty to our ear.

Next, Shakespeare—enough said. Shakespeare and Chaucer would have had to work to converse, but we do not see Shakespeare as having deformed the language of the *Canterbury Tales*. Rather, we might imagine the transformation from Old English to *Hamlet* with stately medieval-style music on the sound track, full of French horns scored in tidy thirds and fourths. From Shakespeare we pass on to the King James Bible, Samuel Johnson's dictionary, Jane Austen, and pretty soon we're home.

All of this is seen as noble, "historical," a matter of our "mighty" and "open" language coming to be. But somehow, there seems to be an idea that the process had an inherent end point, beyond which we are not to go. It's as if somebody somewhere had been endeavoring to meld a chunky Germanic tongue spoken by some restless warrior tribes into precisely the English we have right now, that they officially declared themselves finished sometime not long ago, and that from now on, we are not to mess up their creation.

Obviously, there is a certain arbitrariness here. And here is where the Celtic influence first helps us. The transformation of Old English into Modern English was not, as we have seen, just a matter of new words. The entire grammar changed—and the sky did not fall in. Today we say that we do not "like" nouns being used as verbs: but there was a time when, surely, a lot of people didn't "like" that people were walking around saying things like *Did you see what he's doing?*

We can get an approximate idea of what English would have been like today if the Celts had not saddled English with their "mistakes." English's closest relative is Frisian, a Dutch relative today spoken by some hundreds of thousands in the Netherlands. Frisian, especially since it has lost a goodly number of Proto-Germanic suffixes, can be seen as an approximation of what English might be today if it had not met Welsh and Cornish speakers (or Vikings, but that's the next chapter).

Do we eat apples? in Frisian is *Ite wy appels*? ("Eat we apples?"). No meaningless *do*. If we ask some Frisians with apples in their hands with bites out of them what they're doing, they answer, *Wy ite appels.* They do not specify for us that they are *in the process of eating the apples at this very instant*!!!! As in any normal Germanic language, they would do this only if necessary: *Wy binne oan't iten* ("We're on the eating").

This business of people plugging in an oddly redundant *do* all over the place where it didn't belong, and always sounding oddly caffeinated in describing what they were doing, even though there wasn't even coffee, must have sounded pretty stupid, really, for a long time in England if you weren't born to it. But it caught on, and now it's the only English we know. What was once a mistake is now ordinary. The lesson, quite simply, is that the conception that new ways of putting things are mistakes is an illusion.

———

But—do people perhaps have specific reasons for think-ing that there is something different about our times that made change okay then but anathema now? One senses that when many people look back, they sense that something changed around the mid-1800s. Once we're somewhere between roughly Jane Austen and Nathaniel Hawthorne, English is supposed to stay the way it is ex-cept for new words coming in for new things and old ones dropping out as things go obsolete.

But why just then? What is it about our times that makes English inviolable, whereas in the olden days it was okay for English to morph every which way? Late in rehearsals for the musical *Call Me Madam* in 1950, the writers started to give the star, Ethel Merman, some script changes and she said, "Boys, as of right now I am Miss Birds Eye of 1950: I am frozen. Not a comma!" What is it that made English Miss Birds Eye around a hundred years before *Call Me Madam* opened? Why just then?

Some might answer that in the old old days, English was transformed by various large-scale historical develop-ments that no language could remain unchanged under, such as the Viking and Norman invasions, the genius of Shakespeare, and the general expansion of English into a language suitable for elevated writing styles. Today, one might suppose, English sails along dominating the world, such that suffering the kinds of abbreviations and distortions it did way back when would be—now I'm guessing what the idea might be—beneath the language's dignity? An unnecessary source of confusion that modern education can and should retard?

What that answer misses, however, is that a massive proportion of the way a language changes is a matter of chance, unconnected to words or grammar from other languages or the way the language comes out of the mouths of foreign invaders. Namely, much of what constitutes ordinary Modern English today began as random novelties that floated in, despised as mistakes by the elite.

For example, in the nineteenth century, the time about when so many seem to think English was "done," many grammarians considered the following words and expressions extremely déclassé: *all the time* (quality folks were to say *always*), *born in* (don't you know it's *born at*????), *lit* (What did I tell you, darling? it's *lighted*), *washtub* (I don't know why people can't say *washing tub* as they should!). *Standpoint*, to us a rather cultivated word, was spat upon for supposedly not making sense, since you're not standing anywhere. Believe it or not, it was also considered a tad vulgar to say *Have a look at* instead of *Look at*, and to say *The first two children* instead of *The two first*!! At classier affairs one would also have been advised to avoid popping up with louche vulgarities such as *The house is being built—*

until then, one said *The house is building*—and if you said *stacked* and *fixed* the way we say them instead of "stack-ed" and "fix-ed," to many it sounded like you were *clipping the end of the word*!!

A certain crowd back then were every bit as exercised over those things as so many of us are today over *Billy and me* and singular *they* (they didn't like these either, of course). Yet from our vantage point, these concerns look arbitrary at best and comical at worst—I myself find fusty old complaints about these words and expressions every bit as funny as the late, great television show *Arrested Development*. (*Standpoint*, according to one fellow in 1867, was just "not an English word." Hmm.)

So I hereby make up an English sentence:

Let's have a look at the first two chapters I have excerpted, where we learn about the period when the Cross-Bronx Expressway was being built from the standpoint of people who were born in East Tremont and lived there all of their lives.

To people who prided themselves on their concern with "proper" English 150 years ago, that perfectly innocent sentence would have been a galumphing mess full of "mistakes."

The lesson again: the conception of new ways of

putting things as "mistakes" is an illusion. It reflects nothing but a natural human discomfort with the unfamiliar, as well as a certain degree of the herding instinct, such that "we" speak properly while "they" do not.

Right?

No?

Is it that you can't abide the fact that so many of the "errors" in question strike you as not just new but illogical?

Stop Making Sense

Well, let's *have a look at* that. I get what you mean. *Billy and me went to the store* breaks a rule. Because it's *I* who went to the store, as a subject, *me* is downright illogical. It should be fixed. *They* "is" plural. It means two people. If you're going to start using it to mean one person, then where do you draw the line? Why can't we just start using *we* to mean "you"? Or "asparagus"?

An answer to all of this is one that is not exactly tidy, but urgent nonetheless.

No language makes perfect sense.

That's another way of saying: there is no known language that does not have wrinkles of illogicality here and there. If one is to impose an aesthetic preference upon English or any other language, it cannot be one involving perfect order and endless clean lines, because no language like that has ever been spoken, anywhere, by anyone. Rather, one must revel in disorder. Not chaos, but perhaps the contained disorder of an ideal English garden, where it is considered proper to allow certain plants to ramble here and there, certain flowers to spread, drip, dot, dapple. Call them marks of character.

Pronouns, as it happens, are one of the places where languages tend to drip a bit. Russian, for example, gets weird in the *Billy and me* zone, too. To refer to yourself and someone else, you refer to yourself as "we." So *Me and my wife* is *My s ženoj* ("We and the wife"). (Don't be misled by the chance similarity between English *me* and Russian *my*; Russian's *my* means "we.") This is no "royal" *we*—it is the only way to say it. The *we* usage crept in out of a sense that you are referring to two people of which you are one, which is the definition of *we*-ness, just as we say *Everybody can have **their** own piece of cake* because "everybody" brings to mind lots of people rather than one body. In the same way, in Russian you do not say *He and Ivan went fishing*, but *They and Ivan went fishing*. Russians do not consider *My s ženoj* a mistake: it just is. All languages leak.

In Hebrew and other languages in its Semitic family, there is something that truly makes no damned sense and you just have to deal with it. Adjectives take a feminine ending when used with feminine nouns—no surprise there. Adjectives come after the noun, and so *Mazal tov* ("good luck," "congratulations"), but *Šana tova* ("good year," "Happy New Year"). But for some reason, numbers above two turn it around: they take a feminine ending with masculine nouns and no ending with feminine ones. Kibbutzes are male in Hebrew, and so three kibbutzes: *kibutzim šloša.* Bananas are women, and so three bananas is *bananot šaloš.* This just is. Israelis don't "not like" it. It's been that way forever, it's that way in Arabic, it's just that way. All languages leak.

Or then there's a language in which when, and only when, you use a verb in the third person singular you pin a *z* sound to the end of it. That is, English: the ending is written as an -*s*, but if you think about it, it's usually pronounced as *z*: *tries* (you don't say "trice"), *mows, kills, tars, bids, wags,* and so on. Having a conjugational ending in the present only for the third person singular is vastly rare, believe it or not (I am aware of it in no other language on earth and am not alone among linguists in that), and surely part of the reason is that it doesn't really make sense. What's it there for? Wouldn't the language be more logical if there were just no endings? Notice that this is exactly where many speakers try to take English in their colloquial speech—only to be condemned as making a "grammatical error"!

Which brings us to an idea some might have that even

if all languages to date leak, there isn't anything wrong with trying to make English the first exception. We, after all, do have things like coffee and broccoli and electricity. We had the Enlightenment. Far be it from us to accept the natural as the inevitable, one might say.

But to plug up all of English's holes, you'd have to get rid of a lot more than singular *they*, *Billy and me,* and a few other blips that happen to attract so much attention. For example, what about good old meaningless *do*? It doesn't make a whit of sense. It contributes nothing, and just makes forming negative sentences and questions more involved than it ever was before. Obviously we're stuck with it—no one expects us to start talking like Frisians. *Want you* to stop using meaningless *do*? It's illogical—but we *do* not care. Nor *do* we have much time for splitting hairs over the "logic" of using the progressive marker to express an ordinary present tense that it was not originally used for. We do not, and *can*not, care.

The snippy grammar mavens of yesteryear had their "logical" reasons for "not liking" plenty of other things we now have no problem with. For example, *first two* was thought to connote the first pair of something as opposed to some other pair or trio; otherwise, it was thought that one "should" say *two first*—i.e., to simply refer to the initial two in a sequence with no comparison intended with subsequent pairs or trios. Even today we can see how

that makes a kind of sense—Jane Austen used *two first*—
but we also cannot help sensing it as almost elusively particular. Maybe it'd be kind of nice if we had learned to
fashion that little antimacassar distinction. But unsurprisingly, we didn't, and no one cares today. What's the big
deal about singular *they*, then?

English is shot through with things that don't really
follow. *I'm the only one, amn't I?* Shouldn't it be *amn't* after
all? *Aren't*, note, is "wrong" since *are* is used with *you*, *we*,
and *they*, not *I*. There's no "I are." *Aren't I?* is thoroughly
illogical—and yet if you decided to start saying *amn't* all
the time, you would lose most of your friends and never
get promotions. Except, actually, in parts of Scotland and
Ireland where people actually do say *amn't*—in which
case the rest of us think of them as "quaint" rather than
correct!

When's the last time you learned a language where the
word for *you* was the same in the singular and plural
always? (Note that I have avoided the street-corner putres-
cence of *all the time*!) I don't mean ones where you can
use the plural *you* in addressing one person to be polite
(French *vous*, German *Sie*, etc.)—but ones where *you* really
is the only pronoun available in the second person for
both singular and plural?

There are, believe it or not, languages where pronouns
vary only for person but not number, such that *I* and *we*

are the same word, *he, she,* and *they* are the same word, and as such, singular and plural *you* are the same word. For some reason this tends to be in Indonesia and New Guinea. But for it to be this way only with the second person? Odd, and, again, illogical, inconsistent, unpretty. And as always, when people try to clean it up and make a plural *you* with words like *y'all* and *you'uns* and *y'uns,* they are patronized as "colorful."

The ending *-ly* makes an adjective into an adverb, right? *Strongly, helpfully, badly.* Why, then, does it pop up on adjectives as well? *A portly gentleman,* my hometown Philadelphia *The City of Brotherly Love, an hourly massage* (I wish). It doesn't make sense, but try to clean it up and call Philly a city of "brother-love" and one implies an entirely different affair.

Look at these words:

fiddle	fondle	nibble	riddle	dabble
dribble	diddle	giggle	stipple	tickle
nipple	jiggle	wiggle	trickle	curdle

Notice how they share a certain element in their meanings? All of them have to do with rapid, repetitive movement, a "hummingbird" quality. That means that the *-le* ending is actually a suffix—it carries meaning.

But if so, it's a funny kind of suffix. With other suffixes, the words they are used with can also occur by themselves. *Strongly, strong. Happiness, happy. Curiosity, curious.* But with *-le*, as often as not the original word doesn't exist. There are *nip, jig, dab,* and *curd.* But *nib* hangs around only on the margins of the language: I have used it exactly once in my forty-two-year life and that was at the beginning of this sentence. *Drib* is frozen into the set expression *dribs and drabs* (one does not say, *Look, a drib!*). *Trick,* although obviously a word, is a different one from the one that formed the basis of *trickle* (which does not mean to pull the wool over someone's eyes in twittering repetition!), and in the same way we cannot *fid, fond, did, gig, wig, rid, tick,* or *stip.*

That is illogical. If *wiggle* means to squirm rapidly, then why isn't there a verb to *wig* that refers to the undulating motion of a hula dance? Why doesn't the mighty Mississippi River *trick* majestically along? Why doesn't *tick* mean a seductive caress? Or, why can't we add *-le* to other words? Why are we never described as *knockling* on a door? Why don't we say that a drummer doing a drumroll is *tappling*?

Well, we just don't—but if you want to make English the world's first leakless language, you've got your work cut out for you with what linguists call our *frequentative* suffix *-le.* Which would include imprinting upon the English-speaking world various other words, such as *sprink* and *chort.*

Billy and me, then, is just one more place where English has a wrinkle. In English, when subject pronouns are used after *and*, they are expressed in the form otherwise used for objects, just like in Russian, when you refer to yourself and someone else as a subject, *I* is expressed in the form otherwise used for the first person plural. That's all.

The question is, then, what makes that "error" and the others we hear about so important compared to the ones no one bats an eye about?

Wouldn't it seem that mere accident has people writing things like *I'm correct in viewing the use of* they *in the singular as incorrect,* **aren't** *I*? Or that people who "don't like" *impact* as a verb have no problem with the fact that the word *fun* nonsensically straddles the line between noun and adjective? *A fun party, a long party*—adjectives. *The party was fun, the party was long*—adjectives. But then, *fun* can be a noun: *We had fun, I'm sick of fun*—but "we had long"??? What "part of speech" is *fun*?

It bears mentioning that clarity is not an issue with the "errors" in question. Hearing someone say *Billy and me went to the store*, no one muses, "Hark—who is the person other than Billy that he refers to? I hear no subject!" When Thackeray wrote "A person can't help their birth," no one stopped and wondered "But who's the *other* person????"

The rub is purely the issue of "logic," and the fact is that there are no languages that make perfect sense throughout. After all, a language loping along with a meaningless *do* while dressing up its present tense in progressive clothing sure doesn't. In a perfectly logical English, you would say, **Amn't I the one who have to sprink** *the second coat of paint on?* I presume that you have no desire to say sentences like this.

The Celtic impact on English, then, shows us that truly novel things can happen to the way a language puts words together and yet its speakers will continue to understand one another, and the language can go on to be the vehicle of a great literature.

My experience suggests that at this point, many people will still have trouble shaking a sense that observing these "rules" is part of being a respectable member of society. And it is true that in the reality of the world we live in, we cannot say *Billy and me went to the store* in a formal speech without seeming crude and untutored to many audience members; nor will my arguments change the convictions of those who write house style sheets for copy editors.

I would hope, however, that we might think of these things as what they are: arbitrary fashions of formal language that we must attend to just as we dress according to the random dictates of the fashions of our moment. Remember that what is considered "proper" English varies with the times just as fashion does.

There was a time when pedants hoped that English could pattern like Latin and not end sentences with prepositions. That fashion passed.

There was a time when pedants developed a minor obsession over English's tendency to use expressions like *have a look* and *make a choice* rather than *look* and *choose*. That fashion passed.

In our time, pedants are engaged in a quest to keep English's pronouns in their cages instead of *me* being used as a subject after *and* and *they* being used in the singular. Whether that fashion will pass I cannot say, but we do know that it is nothing but one more fashion. Russians happen to prefer smothering their food in sour cream much more than Americans, and in Russia the space occupied in modern American culture by wine is occupied by vodka. These are cultural differences, distinctions of vogue. Similarly, Russians with their "We and the wife" do not know our *fashion* of policing pronouns to make sure they never venture beyond their original meanings. Today as in the olden days, we are dealing with vogue indeed. People in the seventies did not think sideburns, wide collars, and bell-bottoms were more "logical" than previous fashions. It was just what people were delighted by in a passing sense, then, for a while.

We are taught that these errors are a sign of some possible catastrophe if they are allowed to persist. But I'm not sure people are aware of how languages have a way of holding together. Nothing reminds me of this more than the truly screwed-up English in the funniest book ever written in human history, *The New Guide of the Conversation in Portuguese and English*. It was written in the late 1800s by a Portuguese man described by Mark Twain in the introduction to a latterly printing as an "honest and upright idiot," who neither spoke nor even read English, and was under the impression that he could render English by just plugging English words into French sentences. The book is almost two hundred pages of the likes of this, one of my favorite bits in it, a vignette about fishing called "The fishing":

> That pond it seems me many multiplied of fishes. Let us amuse rather to the fishing.
>
> I do like-it too much.
>
> Here, there is a wand and some hooks.
>
> Silence! There is a superb perch! Give me quick the rod. Ah! There is, it is a lamprey.
>
> You mistake you, it is a frog! Dip again it in the water.
>
> Perhaps I will do best to fish with the leap.
>
> Try it! I desire that you may be more happy and more skilful who a certain fisher, what have fished all day without to can take nothing.

Now, that's errors for you. And notice that no native speaker of English ever sounds anything like this and never has, regardless of *their* attendance to "errors." I have no idea, for example, what "the leap" referred to. I also submit "you mistake you," so marvelously erroneous, as a sample of what "wrong" English really can be, in considering whether modern English speakers are prone in any meaningful way to "errors."

I also submit that that very way of putting it, "you mistake you," leads us into the next chapter. There is a reason why one puts it as "you mistake you" in Portuguese and French—and normal Germanic languages—but not English. It's part of a bigger picture—one with Vikings in it.

Three

WE SPEAK A
BATTERED GRAMMAR

WHAT THE VIKINGS DID TO ENGLISH

English, as languages go, and especially Germanic ones, is kind of easy.

Not child's play, but it has fewer bells and whistles than German and Swedish and the rest. Foreigners are even given to saying English is "easy," and they are on to something, to the extent that they mean that English has no lists of conjugational endings and doesn't make some nouns masculine and others feminine.

There is a canny objection one sometimes hears out there, that English is easy at first but hard to master the details of, while other languages are hard at first but easy to master the details of. Purportedly, then, Russian means starting out cracking your teeth on its tables of conjugations and case markers and gender marking, but after that it's smooth sailing.

Nonsense. English really is easy(-ish) at first and hard later, while other languages like Russian are hard at first and then *just as hard later*! Show me one person who has said that learning Russian was no problem after they mastered the basics—after the basics, you just keep wondering how anybody could speak the language without blacking out. English is truly different. Why?

Not because so many immigrants have learned it, either amid the British slave trade or later in America. We must always ask: in our modern world, how would the way the language is spoken by subordinate people, usually ridiculed as "bad grammar," make its way into how middle-class native-born people spoke, and especially how they wrote? Some words, maybe—but as always, grammar is key. There is the way the Bosnian cabdriver speaks English now—and then there is the way the people on National Public Radio talk. Just how would Zlatko the cabdriver's locutions affect how Terry Gross expresses herself? Obviously, not at all—even if there were millions of Zlatkos.

Besides, English drifted into its streamlined state long before the colonial era, when it was still a language only occasionally written in, and spoken by only some millions of people on a single island. The reason English is easy is a story which, like the Celtic one, traditional linguists have missed most of, in favor of seeing an uncanny number of developments in the same direction as "just happening," though they are unheard-of in any other Germanic language or, often, anywhere on earth.

Namely, the Danes and Scandinavians who invaded and settled Britain starting in the eighth century battered not only people, monasteries, and legal institutions, but the English language itself.

Before we go on, by the way, don't worry that "Germanic" means keeping track of twelve vastly different tongues. Really, just think of it as four.

The first "language" is Swedish, Norwegian, and Danish, sometimes called Mainland Scandinavian. These three are variants of the same language; their speakers can converse.

The second language is Dutch. "Dutch" for us can include Frisian, a close relative, and Afrikaans, which is Dutch after centuries of separate development in South Africa.

The third language is High German. Yiddish is an off-shoot of what also became High German, and is in essence a German dialect with a lot of words from Slavic and Hebrew. Some Yiddish scholars bristle when you say that, but it's true, with all due respect for Yiddish's position in a culture quite separate from the Teutonic one. So you can just think, for our purposes, of "German."

Finally, there is Icelandic. Faroese is so similar to it that you can just think of a general "Icelandic."

That really is all you need: Volvos, Vermeers, Volkswagens, and Volcanoes.

The Tip of the Iceberg:
Suffixes

Traditional scholarship on The History of English recognizes that the Vikings played a part in a single thing that happened to English besides words, words, words. Namely, as we have seen, Old English shed a lot of endings in its day, such that in comparison Middle English seems like one of those nearly hairless cats.

It happened on verbs as well as nouns. Where in Modern English we have *I love, you love, he loves, we love*, where the only ending is the third person one with its *-s*, Old English had *ic luf-ie, þū luf-ast, hē luf-að, wē luf-iað*. (Quick sidebar on something we'll see a lot of in this chapter—nothing hard: in Old English spelling, *þ* was the *th* sound in *thin*, and *ð* was the *th* sound in *this*.)

It is more or less accepted that the Vikings must have had something to do with this. Modern Danish and Norwegian didn't exist yet; rather, the Vikings spoke the ancestor of those languages, an early branch of Proto-Germanic called Old Norse. Old Norse was, like Old English, a language all ajangle with suffixes like Latin.

When the Vikings came, one of their first tasks was to

communicate with the Anglo-Saxons. This was not as tough a proposition for them as the one they would have faced had they invaded Greece. It is assumed that speakers of Old English and speakers of Old Norse could probably wangle a conversation. To ask "Do you have a horse to sell?" an Old English speaker would say *"Haefst þu hors to sellenne?,"* which would have made some kind of sense to an Old Norse speaker since in his language it went *Hefir þu hross at selja?*

Understanding was one thing, but reproducing what he heard was another. For the Old Norse speaker, Old English was familiar but different, kind of like driving on the wrong (I mean, left!) side of the road in England feels to an American at first. Old English had endings in the same places and used in the same ways—but *different* endings. Take the word for "to deem, to judge":

	Old English	*Old Norse*
I	*dēme*	*doemi*
you	*dēmest*	*doemir*
he/she	*dēmeþ*	*doemir*
we	*dēmaþ*	*doemum*
y'all	*dēmaþ*	*doemiþ*
they	*dēmaþ*	*doema*

This was a basically bookless realm, recall, and so a Norseman did not see tables of endings laid out neatly on a page like this, nor did anyone teach him the language formally at all (short of perhaps being told occasional *words*, but that doesn't allow you to express yourself). It was an oral world—people just talked; they didn't write or read. The Norseman just heard these endings being used on the fly. It must have been confusing, and as such, tempting to just leave the endings off when speaking English, since he could be understood without them most of the time. This was the recipe for what eventually became Modern English, where the only remnant of the present-tense conjugations above is the third person singular -*s*, a little smudge left over from ye olde -*th*.

Yet, as always, the ancient world left us no actual descriptions of Vikings making their way in English and how well they did at it. We can infer a little from things like an eleventh-century inscription on a sundial, written in Old English by someone with a Scandinavian name, "Orm Gamalson":

Orm Gamalsuna bohte Sanctus Gregorius minster
tobrocan & tofalan & he hit let macan newan from
grunde . . .

"Orm Gamalson bought St. Gregory's minster broken and fallen down and had it made anew from the ground . . ."

Thus a Scandinavian was writing in English: that's one glimpse at one Viking who wrapped his head around the language. But we'll never know anything about Orm, including how he learned English, much less how he actually rendered it in his everyday speech. And that historiographical lacuna has allowed some linguists to propose that the Orm Gamalsons had nothing to do with English taking it all off.

They point out that Swedish, Norwegian, and Danish have lost almost as many endings as English has, and Dutch and Frisian are not too far behind them. In the present, for example, Swedish and friends even surpass English; here is how to conjugate "to call" in Swedish— i.e., you don't!

jag kallar	*vi kallar*
du kallar	*ni kallar*
det kallar	*de kallar*

But this observation misses the forest for the trees. While other Germanic languages have sloughed off a certain number of endings, they have never done so to the radical degree that English has. For example, the *kallar* conjugation business acknowledged, not a single one of them in Europe does without classifying their nouns according to gender.

Gender, to an American English speaker, is like water fountains. An American in Paris may notice after a while that there are virtually no water fountains: long before bottled water became commonplace in America, having to buy it in Paris was a minor inconvenience that an American had to get used to. However, it was a mistake to think that an absence of water fountains was something particular to Paris, or even France. Water fountains are uncommon in Europe in general; it's America that has been a little odd in having them in such proliferation.

In the same way, an English speaker trying a European language runs up against gender in Spanish's *el sombrero* for *the hat* but *la luna* for *the moon* and thinks of it as something annoying about Spanish, but then will also encounter it in French, Russian, Greek, Albanian, Polish, Welsh even! It's English that is odd in not having gender,[1] even among the Germanic languages.

Proto-Germanic had not one but three genders— masculine, feminine, and neuter—and in some cases modern Germanic languages retain all three, in such user-hostile cases as each piece of silverware in German having

---

1. Indeed, English has what is called biological gender: *actor/actress* and that sort of thing. All languages do. What we lack is what is called grammatical gender— words assigned to "genders" for little or no predictable reason. On biological gender, I can't resist sharing one of my favorite sentences ever, in an article written by a fine but non-native writer: "Like English, Chinese is a language without gender, i.e., apart from the natural sex of the nouns such as *man, woman, boy, waitress, cock, bitch,* etc."

a different gender: spoons are boys, forks are girls, knives are hermaphrodites. Usually, just two genders remain—but remain they do, showing no signs of going anywhere. In Swedish, a big goose is masculine, *en stor gås*, but a big house is what is called common, and comes out *ett stort hus*, where *ett* is the common form for *a* and the adjective takes a common ending *-t*.

English is, as always, the odd one out on this. It is the only genderless Germanic language, except for one dialect of Swedish—but then there is another Swedish dialect, and others in Denmark, that retain all three of Proto-Germanics' genders. *No* modern dialect of English retains gender—not marked on nouns like Spanish's *-o* and *-a* endings, not in the form of distinct articles like Swedish's *en* and *ett*, and certainly not with endings on adjectives. In fact, English is the only Indo-European language in all of Europe that has no gender—the only one.[2]

Here is where we come back to the question as to whether we can usefully say that English's loss of suffixes

---

2. There are, however, genderless Indo-European languages beyond Europe. Armenian has no gender "just because"—but has seven cases (!), and so has hardly undergone an English-style sloughing-off experience. Persian has no gender—but then this is almost definitely because of a drive-by in its history similar to the one English underwent, upon which if you're really interested, if I may be forgiven for plugging myself, see my *Language Interrupted: Signs of Non-Native Acquisition in Standard Language Grammars* (New York: Oxford University Press, 2007). Among Germanic languages, Afrikaans has no gender, but it is Dutch filtered through southern African peoples transforming it in like fashion to, but to a lesser extent than, what Vikings did to English (and thus retains almost everything otherwise that German and the gang do, as we'll see as we go on).

"just happened." If that's all there was to it, why did it happen only to a single Indo-European language in Britain and nowhere else in Europe?

"But Wait, There's More!":
The Rest of the Iceberg

And in any case, the issue goes way beyond endings. There is a great deal more about English that is curiously "easy" as Germanic goes.

This occurred to me several years ago when I was spending a month in Germany, trying to bone up on my vocabulary by reading a German translation of one of my favorite books. I kept trying to maintain the fiction that the only significant difference between German and English is that German has *der, die, das,* and a bunch of endings while all English has is little old *the* and just a few endings. But it just isn't true.

Beyond endings, German grammar is "busier" than English's. You have to watch out for more things, split more hairs. And that's also true of the Scandinavian languages, regardless of their scanty little old verb conjugations. It's true of any Germanic language, from Proto-Germanic on down over these past three thousand years. Except English.

For example, I said that *You mistake you* for *You're mistaken* from the wacky English example would be germane to the Viking issue. What I meant was that the misled Portuguese gentleman thought of *you mistake you* as normal because *you mistake yourself* is the way you put it in French (*Tu te trompes*) and Portuguese (*Tu te equivocas*) (both meaning "You 'yourself' mistake").

This is a quirk common in European languages, that often you do things "to yourself" which in English you just do. It tends to be with verbs having to do with moving and feeling. So in English, *I have to go,* but in Spanish, *Tengo que irme* ("I have to go 'myself' "). With moving, this makes a kind of sense to an English speaker, although it seems a little redundant to us to have to specify that I am exerting the act of *go*-age upon *myself*. But the ones involving feelings are something else: *I remember* in English, *Me acuerdo* in Spanish ("I remember myself"), meaning not that you are idly recalling a past image of yourself, but that the remembering is something that happens to you, thus affecting not something or someone else, but you. While about the only Modern English versions of these are *behave yourself,* to *perjure yourself,* and *to pride yourself* (*upon*), many European languages mark hundreds of verbs in that way.

It's a frill—a language doesn't need to mark that things obviously personal in fact—Golly!—involve the person in question. But some languages just do, especially in Europe. Germanic languages are included: in German *You mistake you* comes out as *Du irrst **dich*** ("You mistake yourself"), and *to remember* is *sich erinnern*. In Frisian, if I am ashamed, *Ik skarnje **my*** ("I shame me"); to have the same feeling in Iceland is to *skammast **sín**,* or among Yiddish speakers to *shemen **zikh**.* In Dutch, one does not just *move,* one *bewegt **zich*** ("moves oneself"). In Swedish to move is similar: *röra **sig**.*

All of this would have been same-old same-old to an Old English speaker. Today's *behave yourself* and *pride yourself* are fossils from a time when, for example, if I was afraid *Ic ondrēd mē*, i.e., in a way, "bedreaded myself," and to look at something was to, as it were, "besee oneself to" it: *Beseah he **hine** to anum his manna* ("Looked he himself to one of his men"). But over a few centuries in Middle English documents, we watch this "self"-fetish mysteriously blow away like autumn leaves. Today it is gone, while alive and well in all the other Germanic languages.

To strike an archaic note, in English we start popping off *hithers* and *thithers*. Come *hither*, go *thither*, but stay *here* or stay *there*. *Hither, thither,* and *whither* were the "moving" versions of *here, there,* and *where* in earlier English. It's something you still have to pick up in German: "Where's the coffee?" *Hier.* But *Come here!* is *Komm her!* *"Komm hier"* marks the foreigner; I'll just bet that's one of the things Germans say to imitate English speakers' schoolboy German. German also has its *thither* (*hin*) and *whither* (*wohin*), and in fact there is no Germanic language that has no directional adverbs of this kind. These are *Germanic* languages, after all: precise, specific!

But one Germanic language doesn't care so much about dotting *i*'s and crossing *t*'s. And it used to. Old English had a good old-fashioned trio: *hider, þider,* and *hwider*. These were passed down into Middle English as *hither, thither,* and *whither*. But they eventually blew away like autumn leaves. Today they are gone.

Quite a few European languages have a word that refers to people in a generic sense. Spanish's *Se habla español* is the most familiar example: *se* here means "you" in the sense of "one." In French this is *on*. In German it is *man*: *Hier* (not *her!*) *spricht man Deutsch* ("One speaks German here"). As it is in most of the other Germanic languages (an exception is that in Icelandic the word for *men, maður,* subs for *man*). This means that in Germanic languages there is almost always a nice, filled-out array of pronouns making lots of distinctions, like in Swedish:

jag "I"	*vi* "we"
du "you"	*ni* "y'all"
han, hon, det "he, she, it"	*de* "they"
man "one"	

In comparison, English settles for making poor *you* do an awful lot of work:

I	we
you	**you**
he, she, it	they
you	

Notice that while Swedish has its *"se habla"* pronoun *man*, in English we drag *you* in to do that job: ***You*** *have to be careful with these big corporations.* In Old English, though, there was a *man* pronoun, too. But in Middle English documents, over three hundred years it blows away like autumn leaves. Today it is gone.

Learn a European language, including any Germanic language but Swedish, and note that quite often, while most verbs form their past perfect with the verb *have*—*Ich habe gesprochen* ("I have spoken")—a good little bunch do it with the verb *be*, too—*Ich bin gekommen* ("I 'am come'"). Just like in Old English: *Learning had fallen away* was "Learning *was* fallen away": *Lār āfeallen wæs.*

Marking some verbs with *be* instead of *have* is a matter of being explicit about a certain nuance: in the perfect, the verbs marked with *be* refer, technically, to a state rather than an action; i.e., something that *be*s. When you say you have arrived, you mean that you have now achieved the state of being there: "I'm here, so let's get started." On the other hand, when you talk about how you raked leaves this afternoon, you usually are getting across that you *per-*

formed the action of raking leaves, not that you have achieved the *state* of having raked the leaves and are now ready to have your picture taken.

We English speakers think, "Well, yeah . . ." but hardly feel it necessary to split that hair. The other Germanic languages do split it—and Old English did.

But something strange started happening in Middle English, as usual; now it was the *be*-perfect that was falling away (like autumn leaves). By Shakespeare, *be* is used with only a few verbs ("And didst thou not, when she **was** gone downstairs, desire me to be no more so familiarity with such poor people?" *Henry IV, Part II*, II, i, 96) and today, it lingers on only in a frozen form such as *The autumn leaves now are gone*. Even there, you may well have thought of *gone* as an adjective (*The leaves are red, The leaves are gone*), and in any case you can also say *The autumn leaves **have** gone*, which, in this case of the grand old Old English *be*-perfect, they have, as always in English.

In any self-respecting member of the Germanic family, one (*man?*) puts the verb in the second slot in the sentence, hell or high water. So for *I saw a film*, German has *Ich sah einen Film*—nothing odd there. But if you want to say *Yesterday I saw a movie*, "saw" has to stay in that second slot, and so "I" has to come after it: *Gestern sah ich einen Film* ("Yesterday saw I a film"). The verb sits tight in that second slot and everything else has to manage. In all the

Germanic languages it has to be "Yesterday saw I . . ." to keep the verb in second place. Swedish for *Today she's driving the car* has to be:

> *I dag kører hun bilen*
> today drives she the car

which gets *kører* ("drives") into that number two slot after *I dag* ("today").

This quirk of word order, which linguists call "verb-second" or "V2" for short, is by no means common in the world, and to my knowledge is only a family trait today in Germanic, in which it is as normal as Apfel pie. The details differ from language to language, but all Germanic languages have it—except one. Its absence in that one (guess which one!!) is odd. Although, given that the one it is absent from also shucked off so much else, maybe it's not odd. Maybe there is a reason behind all of this.

English's autumnal leaf-dropping quality involves even more cases,[3] but I need not list them all: you get

---

3. For those who care, in "normal" Germanic languages: you say "She washed me the hair" rather than *She washed my hair* when talking about things done to your person; there remains alive a bouquet of prefixes that are long dead or fossilized in English, like *be-* (*bedecked*) and *for-* (*forbear*—did you ever think about what *for-* "means"?); the word *become* is used to mark the passive voice instead of just *be*; there is a pronoun especially for singular *you* like English's *thou* now gone in the standard dialect; and then on top of that lots of endings are retained, such as to mark adjectives or the subjunctive.

the point. No Germanic language has shed as much of what Proto-Germanic passed down to it as English, by a long shot. Of course some drop a stitch here and there more than others. Afrikaans has no gender, because it is what happened when Dutch was learned by so many Africans that, unlike any Germanic language on the Continent, it went as far as English did and lost gender. However, in terms of the many other features that make a language a descendant of Proto-Germanic, Afrikaans is very much a card-carrying member: in Afrikaans, you "remember yourself," you come *hither*, there is a nice *man* pronoun, a *be*-perfect, and the V2 tic. Swedish, as noted, has lost its *be*-perfect (although it holds on in Norwegian and Danish). However, Swedish is otherwise as Germanic as, well, German.

English's grammar, then, is "easier" than the other Germanic languages'. The Grand Old History of English describes these "difficult" features as just mysteriously melting away. But none of these authors have had occasion to consider how very *many* such features just melted away, and that nothing similar was happening in other Germanic languages. The question beckons: why has English been so strangely prone to just letting it all go?

Back in the twenties, pioneering linguist Edward Sapir groped at the question in an elegantly put discussion of the *whither/hither/thither* case:

They could not persist in live usage because they
impinged too solidly upon the circles of meaning
represented by the words *where*, *here* and *there*. That
we add to *where* an important nuance of direction
irritates rather than satisfies.

Sapir's writing, as always, satisfies—but it does leave a
question as to why, oh why, speakers of this and only this
Germanic language found nuance so irritating. Scholarship on English has proceeded with about as little interest in that question as Sapir evidently had. Yet the
question has an answer. It's as much a part of the story of
the English language as Chaucer and Caxton.

Whodunit?

When I was about eight, I remember letting a neighborhood friend take a spin on my bike. He was a more
highly spirited fellow than me and gave it a good zip up
and down hills, bumping it down some curbs, doing
"pop-a-wheelies" and so on. Finally he skidded to a stop
in front of me and some of our pals. We heard some screw
or washer from somewhere in the bike clink to the ground.
Then, a pedal fell off, followed by the handlebars. The
seat screws went loose and the seat tipped limply forward,
and finally the back wheel fell out. My friend ended up
squatting on a mangled heap of bars and gears, and we

and our friends watching howled with laughter for the next fifteen minutes.

I swear I remember this, and yet upon reflection I can't help suspecting that the memory has been distorted in my mind over time. After all, bicycles do not just fall to pieces like that—it would be like something out of a Looney Tune. Maybe something happened just to the seat, or just a wheel slipped—but with all due acknowledgment of entropy, the bike cannot have completely disintegrated right under him. Why, after all, would a bike do that?

Languages are no more likely to toss off massive amounts of grammatical features than bikes are to fall to dust. For example, in language groups other than Germanic, there is never one language that just miraculously becomes a stripper. Supposedly, what happened to English is so unremarkable. But the 250 languages of Australian Aborigines are known for having lots of suffixes, and even though the languages have been spoken there for several tens of thousands of years, not a single one has drifted into a state like English's.

What this means is that something happened to English. Someone did something to it. If a bike does collapse under its rider, then we know that earlier that day, somebody loosened all of its screws so that it would fall apart after being ridden hard for a while. Somebody unscrewed English. Attention must be paid.

John McWhorter

Let's pay some, and line up the suspects. It has, actually, been bruited about that English was turned into a simpler language by the Norman French. The idea is tempting, but impossible. There were, for one, never all that many Normans on the ground in England—one estimate is about ten thousand amid a British population of one or two million. The Normans were an elite living amid masses of ordinary people speaking English as they always had. Thus, even if Normans tended to speak English in an inaccurate way, there is no reason that English-speaking folk would imitate them—if they ever even met them.

This even includes people as influential as the kings of England who, for a while, were men of Norman birth who likely did not even speak English. Think about it— let's imagine that the king does speak English, but as a second language, like, say, Maurice Chevalier. You, on the other hand, talk like Eric Idle. If you ever actually heard the king speak—and that's a big "if," especially since there's no radio or TV—no matter what esteem you hold the king in, why would you start walking around talking like him, so consistently that your children hear you talking only that way? If by chance you really were so odd a person, what would the chances be that whole villages would take to doing what you were doing, 24/7, for a century?

Besides, evidence suggests that the Normans didn't speak funny English for long anyway. By a hundred years and change after the Battle of Hastings in 1066, there are reports of Normans needing to have French taught formally to their children, and of people of Norman ancestry speaking good English like anyone else. By the early 1300s, William of Nassyngton famously had it that:

> And somme understonde wel Englysch
> that can nother Latyn nor Frankys.
> Bothe lered and lewed, olde and gonge,
> Alle understonden english tonge.

Lewed, by the way, meant "unlearned"—neat how the word has evolved into its modern *Hustler* connotation. And *gonge*, by the way, was *young*.

We can assume, then, that the Norman impact on English was in terms of words, and lots of them. That's old news. Who beat up English's *grammar*?

The Viking Impact

Here is where our Vikings come in. Grown men raised on Old Norse were suddenly faced with having to do their raggedy best speaking *Englisc* on a regular basis whenever they spoke with anyone besides the guys they came over with. The simple fact is that adults have a harder time learning languages than children and teenagers—and this was an era when there was no Berlitz, no language instruction beyond someone on the fly telling you, "Here's the word for . . . ," and for the most part, not even any writing.

They came in one wave after another over a century—
for generations there were ever new hordes of men from
across the sea not speaking the language right. Crucially,
whereas French came to England as an elite language
spoken by rulers living remotely from the common folk,
the Vikings took root on the ground, often marrying
English-speaking women, such that their children actually
heard quite a bit of their "off" English. All of this had an
effect on the English language.

The waves in question started in 787, Danes on the
eastern side and Norwegians round the western one. For
the next hundred years England coped with increasing
numbers of these invaders, culminating in an agreement
in 886 that the Vikings would confine their dominion to
the northern and eastern half of England, thence termed
the Danelaw.

The power that the Vikings wielded is clear in traditionally noted things such as the proliferation of Scandi-
navian-derived place names in the Danelaw area ending
in *-by* and *-thorp*, and names ending in *-son* (like Orm Gamalson, he of the sundial), as well as transformations of
bureaucratic procedure. These things alone, however,
cannot, in the strict sense, tell us much about whether these
people were passing their rendition of English down to new
generations of people of both Scandinavian and Anglo-
Saxon (and Celtic) descent. Power can be wielded by

almost counterintuitively small numbers of people, and thus have no effect on how everyday language is spoken.

For example, China was ruled by foreigners for much of its history, including the famous Mongolian regime of Genghis Khan, as well as Manchus from 1644 to as recently as 1911. However, the languages of the rulers had no effect on Chinese. The foreigners ruled from their compounds, using interpreters to communicate with the outside. Actual Chinese people largely encountered the foreigners in occasional interactions with soldiers—if at all. Chinese as spoken by millions across a vast land was unaffected.[4] In Africa, colonial languages, like English, French, and Portuguese, have certainly poured words into small local languages—but they have had almost no effect on these languages' grammars. How one uses the *grammar* in, say, Chichewa in Malawi has nothing to do with the English Malawians learn in school and see in the movies.

As such, even the fact that the very king of England was Danish for a spell (Cnut, from 1016 to 1035) can tell us nothing as to whether his native Old Norse had any

---

4. There have been arguments that Chinese grammar was affected by the languages of its foreign rulers (most prominently some work by Mantaro Hashimoto). I find this hard to support, and highly suspect that most evaluators would agree with me in light of advances in the study of language contact since Hashimoto wrote. I present an alternate analysis of the history of Chinese grammar (indeed based on contact, but long before Genghis Khan and the Manchus) in *Language Interrupted: Signs of Non-Native Acquisition in Standard Language Grammars* (New York: Oxford University Press, 2007)(sorry for plug number two).

significant effect upon the *grammar* of English as spoken by everyday people. What we need is evidence that Scandinavians speaking incomplete English would have been so common that children would have heard this faulty rendition as much as, if not more than, regular English— to the extent that "foreigner" English affected what they grew up using as everyday speech.

Imagining this requires putting on our "antique" glasses: children in this era did not go to school, did not read, and there was no "standard English" that they encountered in the media, because in ordinary daily life there was no media to speak of. To children in Anglo-Saxon Britain, language was something you heard people around you—and no one else—speaking. You didn't see it on the page. In getting a sense of how in such a setting the Vikings would have passed on their rendition of English to the ages (and, eventually, to the page you are reading), three things are useful.

First, in many places they were quite densely concentrated: in some parts of the Danelaw most people were of Danish ancestry. This means that "Scandi"-sounding English would have been a matter of not just the occasional Dane or Norwegian here and there ("Mommie, hwy spæketh he like thæt?"),[5] but a critical mass of people.

Second, in documents, we clearly see that English

---

5. This is a mock sentence.

gets simpler first in the north—where the Scandinavians were densely settled. Old English came in at least four dialects. The one usually written in was West Saxon, which is to us today "normal" Old English. But one of the dialects spoken in the Danelaw region was Northumbrian. In Northumbrian toward the end of Old English, as the Battle of Hastings was looming, the conjugational endings were already wearing out, as if someone were having trouble keeping them apart. Sometimes, all the endings in the present tense except the first person singular were the same, *-as*. This is Old English? And by Middle English, in the north, this erosion continued—in the plural the final consonant flaked away, leaving a mere *-e*:

	West Saxon	Northumbrian	Northern Middle English
I	dēme	-o	-e
you	dēmest	-es /-as	-es
he/she	dēmeþ	-es / -as	-es
we	dēmaþ	-as	-e
y'all	dēmaþ	-as	-e
they	dēmaþ	-as	-e

But take a look at what Southern Middle English was still like, where there had been no Vikings—normal Old English:

	Old English	*Southern Middle English*
I	dēme	-e
you	dēmest	-st
he/she	dēmeþ	-þ
we	dēmaþ	-eþ
y'all	dēmaþ	-eþ
they	dēmaþ	-eþ

So it's not that the endings just fell apart all over England out of some kind of guaranteed obsolescence. They fell apart in a particular place—where legions of foreigners were mangling the tongue!

It was the same with gender: it starts flaking away in Northumbrian Old English, while down south all three genders held on possibly into Middle English. Even as recently as the late nineteenth century, rural folk in the extreme southwest in Dorset were still dividing things between a "personal" and an "impersonal" gender. "Personal" things were not only people but all living things and, for some reason, tools. So, of a tree, *He's a-cut down.* But of water, *It's a-dried up.* Even demonstratives still came in two genders: *this water* was impersonal, but in the personal one, said *theäse tree.* Also, the V2 rule started unwinding, predictably, in the north; it held on in the south, including in Kent in the southeast, for much longer.

Finally, our friend Orm Gamalson even left us a crucial window into English as rendered by speakers of Old Norse. Gamalson was writing in the Northumbrian dialect, in which noun suffixes were as much a mess as the verb ones were. In other dialects of Old English, when one wrote of something happening on a ship, *ship* was in the dative and took an *-e* ending: *scipe*. But in Northumbrian, one just said *in scip*: the *-e* was gone. In the same way, in Gamalson's inscription, as it goes on from where we left off with it earlier, he places the rebuilding of the minster "in King Edward's days," which he wrote as *in Eadward dagum*. There are two interesting things about those three words.

First, Orm left off the possessive ending. Just as today, in other Old English sources *Eadward* would take an *-s* suffix to indicate the possessive: *in Eadwardes dagum*. In Orm's part of England people were leaving off endings— but not elsewhere. Orm's part of England was, also, where, well, Orm was. It was Scandi-land, where people not raised in English were speaking it as part of the everyday routine, leaving the niceties off.

But second, the *-um* suffix on *dagum* is revealing. It is a dative plural, and in Northumbrian, this solid suffix hangs on even while the others are wearing away in cases like *scip* for *scipe* and *Eadward* for *Eadwardes*. Even as the Old English era is winding down and even in other Old English dialects, this *-um* suffix is starting to undergo natural wear and tear and morph into the likes of *-en*, in Northumbrian it's always right there as *-um*, shining like a star.

And there's a reason. You can see it in this table. We come back to Old English's *stān* for *stone*, and *armr* in Old Norse meant (get ready . . . !) "arm":

	Old English		Old Norse	
	singular	*plural*	*singular*	*plural*
nominative	stān	stānas	armr	armar
genitive	stānes	stāna	arms	arma
dative	stāne	stān**um**	armi	arm**um**
accusative	stān	stānas	arm	arma

Notice that, usually, Old Norse's endings are different from Old English's. An Orm Gamalson learning English found a little stumbling block almost every time he started to use a noun. But—the dative plural was one of the only places he got a break: the *-um* suffix was one of the only ones that Old English and Old Norse happened to have in common.

It was predictable, then, that people like Orm Gamalson had a way of holding on to -*um* for dear life as the rest of the noun endings burned off: it was familiar to them from Old Norse. The persistence of -*um* only in the Northumbrian dialect, then, was a calling card from the Vikings.

Why Not the Celts?

In terms of dotting our *i*'s and crossing our *t*'s, we must assess whether another group of people speaking something other than English were the ones who beat the grammar up. If the Celts gave English meaningless *do* and progressive -*ing*, then maybe they also, as non-native speakers, knocked off the bells and whistles, right? After all, if they added things like *do*, then why wouldn't they, speaking "*Englisc*" as a second language, also leave off endings and such? This is, in fact, the opinion of the small school of linguists arguing for the Celtic impact.

The problem with this idea is that, as we have seen, the eclipse of endings correlates so perfectly with just where Vikings settled. If the Celts were responsible, then the endings would have dropped away throughout England, or at least in regions where Celts, rather than Vikings, were more densely settled. They did not. Rather, where something is clearly traceable to Celtic, it is a Celtic construction being *added* to English, such as meaningless *do* and the Northern Subject Rule.

According to theory on what happens when languages encounter one another, this negative evidence re the Celts is just what we would expect.

The Celts had a different experience with English than the Vikings did. The Vikings settled and coped with English, and all indications are that Old Norse in England lasted not much longer than the first generation of invaders. History records no enclaves in England where Old Norse was spoken for generations after the invasions. The Vikings spread themselves out, and wherever an Orm Gamalson settled down, what was se habla'ed was English—and Orm's children likely had the same orientation toward Old Norse as Jewish immigrants' children in America in the twentieth century had toward Yiddish. Old Norse was the Old Country; English was the native tongue—cool, in a word. The difference between then and now was that for Orm, Jr., writing was an elite, marginal decoration in daily life; he likely never went to anything we would call school. As such, the "off" English of his dear old Hagar-the-Horrible Dad was what he spoke, too. This was the root of the curiously simplified Germanic language I am writing in.

In contrast, Welsh and Cornish were spoken in England long before the Angles and Co. came, and lived on beside English for a millennium plus. Celtic and English have been set on a long, slow Crock-Pot simmer with one another in the mouths of bilinguals over all of that time. This stewing phenomenon has a technical name: *linguistic equilibrium,* as granted it since the nineties by linguist R. M. W. Dixon.

In situations like this, as a group slowly picks up a new language over centuries but continues to use its native one more usually, they do not simplify the new language. Rather, they season it with constructions they are used to, but otherwise learn that new language fine. The two languages stew together. Soon, the language they are learning looks a little like their native one.

One sees this all over the world. Because of high rates of intermarriage between groups, the aboriginal languages of Australia as well as of South America tend to be deeply mixed with one another in terms of grammar. One language's endings will pattern like the ones from the language spoken down the river, even though the languages are not closely related. Another language will belong to a group where verbs come at the end of a sentence, but its verbs come in the middle because the languages of another group down in the valley are like that, and on and on. Clearly, the people have been learning one another's languages since time immemorial. But—none of the languages are "broken down" or streamlined in the way that English is, compared with its Germanic family members. The languages stewed—they did not boil down.

It's the same in other situations. In India, the Indo-Aryan languages (Hindi, Gujarati, Bengali) and Dravidian languages (Tamil, Telugu) have been stewing for millennia—but none are particularly simplified. African languages like Xhosa and Zulu inherited click sounds from nearby Khoisan languages—more stewing over long periods. Yet Xhosa and Zulu are decidedly not simple. This is part of the South African constitution in Zulu, namely, the sentence "We recognize the injustices of our past": *Siyakukhumbula ukucekelwa phansi kwamalungelo okwenzeka eminyakeni eyadlula*. We don't need to break that down to see that there's nothing precisely user-friendly about Zulu (and the *c* in *ukucekelwa* is a click sound!).

Linguistic equilibrium is what happened between the Anglo-Saxons and the Celts. Celts blanketed the land and had done so forever. Suddenly they were dealing with bands of marauding Germanic speakers, who ended up never leaving. Life changed, but the land remained blanketed with Celts being the Celts they had always been. The Celt could still use their Welsh or Cornish with the people around them whom they had always known—there was no "genocide," after all. Over generations, the flavor of Welsh and Cornish bled into their way of speaking *Englisc*—not just in words, but in grammar. The result after a while was that the typical Celt could speak English just fine—but with a Celtic infusion in the grammar. That was Chapter One. But meaningless *do* and progressive *-ing* are complications, not simplifications. They are stewings.

Many scholars arguing for Celtic influence suppose that Celts would have had particular trouble with English in places where Old English had something in its grammar that Celtic did not. For example, Welsh does not have case marking on its nouns. There are those who assume that this meant that Welsh speakers would have been inclined to omit them when speaking Old English. This is reasonable on its face, but it isn't what happens in situations of linguistic equilibrium. People amid linguistic equilibrium learn the new language just fine, even the hard stuff.

For example, in China, there are dialects of Mandarin developed by speakers of languages of a different family, Altaic (the shop-window rep is Turkish, but the family stretches far, far eastward). Altaic speakers were encroached upon gradually by Mandarin speakers over long periods. Mandarin is a tonal language—tone is part of how you tell one word from another. Altaic languages do not have tone. The exotic Mandarin dialects created by Altaic speakers dealing with Mandarin-speaking newcomers have Altaic word order and other grammatical features from Altaic—but they also all use tones just as Mandarin does, despite how hard tones are to learn. That is, speakers of tone-free Altaic languages learned thoroughly decent Mandarin, including the tones, while seasoning it with some Altaic things they were used to.

In the same way, the Celts would have seasoned English, but otherwise *learned* it, including English cases even if, say, Welsh had none. The Celts' impact on English was what we saw in Chapter One. In this chapter, we must focus on other people.

The Big Picture

As with the Celtic influence on English, we must *deduce* what the Vikings did to English. No one was on-site chronicling how the language was changing decade by decade. Orm Gamalson might record that a minster was "tobrocan & tofalan"—broken and fallen down—but kings, monks, bureaucrats, and scribes in ancient England, to whom writing was *scripture* rather than scribbling, hadn't the slightest inclination to get down on paper for posterity observations of the likes of "Yon Vikinges Englisc is most tobrocan & tofalan!"

Comparison reveals what was going on even if no one at the time bothered to describe it. Among Germanic languages, Icelandic, spoken on a remote island, has (1) rarely been learned by foreigners and (2) is also the least simplified member of the family. Even today, its grammar is so little changed from Old Norse that Icelanders can read the epic *eddas* in Old Norse written almost a thousand years ago. Icelandic has three genders; most of those case endings and conjugations we saw in Old Norse are still used in everyday language in Reykjavík; and it's got the "you mistake you" quirk, hithering and thithering, V2, a *be*-perfect, and most everything else the well-dressed Proto-Germanic descendant wears.

Icelandic shows that there is nothing inevitable about a language tossing off its suffixes and what linguist and anthropologist Edward Sapir called "nuance" over time. Linguists call a language that has a way of holding on to what is passed down to it "conservative." Ordinarily, languages' grammars are rather conservative—like Latin, Greek, and Russian.

In comparison, even the other Germanic languages besides Icelandic are less conservative. It surely isn't an accident that they also, roiling around on the Continent, where populations have been mixing and conquering one another forever, have been learned by foreigners much more than Icelandic. This is why German, Dutch, and Swedish have shed a lot more of Proto-Germanic's suffixes than Icelandic. However, that's pretty much all. Suffixes—small and usually pronounced without stress (or, in the term more common among laymen, accent)—are uniquely fragile. But otherwise, these languages retain the other complexities of Proto-Germanic. Largely, their coexistence with other languages (including one another) has been a matter of linguistic equilibrium—stewing, but not boiling down.

English, in this light, is the odd one out, and what distinguishes it from its relatives is that it underwent marauding hordes of Vikings who never went home, and proceeded to speak the language, as they did so much else, Their Way. They never wrote down that they were doing so—most of them couldn't write anyway. But Icelandic stands as virtual confirmation that adult learners screwing things up was a key factor in how English came to be the way it is. The people who can still read ancient sagas live on a remote, undisturbed island. The people whose language became the most user-friendly member of the family live on an island nearer the Continent, that was, due to that proximity, lustily disturbed by invading migrants.

The Establishment View

There is no body of traditional objections to the claim that Vikings remodeled English grammar, for the simple reason that the claim has not been made in any sustained way. There is a wan kind of acceptance that Vikings had something to do with one thing: the decay of the suffixes. But even here, most writers mention it only in passing, and as we have seen, there are those who deny even this and argue that the decay "just happened." And otherwise, it is accepted that English lost all of the other Proto-Germanic frills just by chance.

One reason this seems plausible to so many linguists is that they think the suffixes and maybe another thing or two are all English has lost from what Proto-Germanic passed down to it. The specialization endemic to modern academia means that few of these scholars do their work with grammar sketches of all of the Germanic languages and their histories in their heads, much less of languages around the world. They write mostly about English alone and, as often as not, just single features of its grammar.

One scholar, for example, looks at how the "you mistake you" kind of sentence flakes away throughout Middle English, and announces that among Germanic languages, English has "an individual tendency to treat overt reflexivity as redundant." But charting this as a mere "individual tendency" means stipulating that this eclipse happened in just one out of a dozen-plus languages, all the others of which were quite happy to require speakers to be utterly redundant in specifying that fear, remembrance, anger, and the like are something involving *yourself* just like washing and shaving are. To this scholar, for this to have happened by chance seems plausible because it's only one thing. But we have to pull back the camera: "you mistake you" is only one of a dozen "individual tendencies" in English in the same direction. She is certainly aware of the loss of suffixes—but that means she thinks it's just a matter of *two* things.

Then other scholars see something flaking away in Middle English and propose an ad hoc explanation, without addressing the fact that the explanation is contradicted by all the other Germanic languages. One writer describing the eclipse of the generic pronoun *man* opines that when it morphed into a shorter form pronounced "muh," it was "too weak" to survive—which leads to the question as to why weak forms even in English like *y'* for *you* (*Y'know?*) will be with us forever, or why similarly "weak" short pronouns in all the other Germanic languages have been holding on for a thousand years.

Or, one of the History of English stars I generally swoon to falls into what I regard as a rare lapse, describing step by step how English became the only Indo-European language in Europe without gender, and analyzing it as a "cumulative weighting of 'decisions' in favour of natural gender." By "natural gender" he means biological gender (e.g., *actor/actress*) as opposed to the random kind of gender that assigns sex to silverware in German and operated in similar fashion in Old English. But the question is *why* English underwent the effect of this "cumulative weighting" while none of the other Germanic languages— and all but a few languages in all of Europe—did.

Then there is the idea that even if English has lost

some features, it has stayed at par in complexity with the other Germanic languages by developing new ones. Here, the problem is that the traditional scholars are not aware of how very much Proto-Germanic equipment English has tossed off. They do not realize what a long road English would have to travel to give German a run for its money the way Old English did.

What they think brings English back to par with German and the rest is, for example, the tricky English future tense. Future tense marking in English is a highly subtle affair, much more so than in other Germanic languages. Could you explain what the difference in meaning is between *I will go*, *I'm going to go*, and *I'm going*? They are not just interchangeable ways of expressing futurity. Try this: you tell someone that you've always wanted a pair of argyle socks and they say, "Okay, tomorrow we'll buy you some." Now, imagine if they said instead, "Okay, tomorrow we're going to buy you some." Notice how that second sentence has a different meaning—it sounds vaguely confrontational. Nobody taught you that—it's a subtlety of English grammar. It's hard, this English future— I am so thankful I learned it from the cradle. A non-native speaker I knew whose English was truly spectacular once said when I asked her age, "I turn twenty-five." Mmm, not quite. It has to be "I'm turning twenty-five." Only if you started with a time expression could you use the bare verb: "Tomorrow I turn twenty-five." Subtle—or, to a non-native, hard.

But this does not make English as grammatically complex as German or any other Germanic language, nor would another thing or two. This is first because English is a good dozen or more features behind the other languages, not just two or three. And then, on top of this, new little complexities have crept into the other Germanic languages as well, as happens to all languages.

In German, one example is a passel of little words that convey nuances of personal attitude. Using them is indispensable to sounding like an actual human being in the language—and mastering them is possible only via a year or more's exposure to the spoken language. *Do you have your socks?* is, in a vanilla sense, *Hast du deine Socken?* But you can also stick in the word *auch—Hast du auch deine Socken?*—in which case the sentence conveys "You have your socks, don't you?" In this usage, *auch* conveys a subtle, personal note of warning, impatience, correction—and there are a bunch of little words in German with subtle, untranslatable meanings of this kind (e.g., *schon, eben, doch, mal,* etc.).

In Swedish and Norwegian, it's tone—the comic lilt that we often use to imitate these languages is not only a matter of a cute "accent," but also conveys what words mean. In Swedish, *anden* can mean two things. Say it in

the way that feels most natural to an English speaker—
AHN-den—and it means "the duck." Say it with a certain
lilt impossible to convey on the page but not a mere
"Swedish chef" singsong, more like sliding down the
"ahn," then leaping up higher onto the "den," and then
dropping off a bit (something like "ah$_n$-DE$_n$"), and it
means "spirit."

All the Germanic languages have morphed into quirks
of this kind, while also retaining so much more of their
core Proto-Germanic equipment than English. English
may be at a certain point along the complexity scale, and
may inch a bit ahead now and then, but the rest of Germanic will always be several steps ahead—in Icelandicness
plus their own driftings into further complexity. For example, linguists also often parry a claim that English is
"easy" by mentioning what we call in this book meaningless *do*. But that's only one more thing, and it was a copy
from Welsh and Cornish, not something that morphed
into the grammar on its own.

Finally, something else that obscures the Vikings' responsibility for English's undressing is the old issue of *scripture*
versus writing. To the traditional History of English specialist, what would show that the Vikings did more to
English than shave off its endings would be if as far back

as Old English—or more precisely, the dialects of Old English spoken in the Danelaw, like Northumbrian and Mercian—right around A.D. 800, *I feared myself* started being rendered as *I am afraid*, *hither* and *thither* dropped out of usage, V2 and the generic *man* pronoun were unknown, and all perfects were expressed with *have* instead of *be*. Instead, as we have seen, in Old English, all we see is the endings eroding. The other things start appearing only in Middle English, and fall away gradually.

But in a world where writing was really scripture, this is what we would expect. The way Vikings rendered English sounded at first, to anyone without Scandinavian ancestry, "other" at best and "wrong" at worst. People writing Old English, poised to engrave the high, "proper" language on the page, would have been loath to waste ink on what they would have regarded as come-as-you-are colloquialisms that not all people use. Only after the post–Norman Conquest blackout of written English, when institutional memory of fashions in how one *scribed* the language had dissolved, would people allow themselves to put a more honest version of the language on paper. That is, what appears to be a stepwise evaporation of Proto-Germanic features in Middle English is actually a record of writers' increasing comfort with putting things in writing that had happened to the language before the Norman Conquest.

Apparently, one feature, the erosion of suffixes, was something that had a way of creeping into the writing even of Anglo-Saxon scribes committed to presenting the language in its Sunday best. Thus we see the suffixes already falling off rapidly in the northeasterly dialects Vikings were exposed to. Suffixes, after all, are little. Using one rather than another does not always feel terribly disruptive. Do you say *roofs* or *rooves*? Whichever you prefer, does the alternative you "don't like" sound *foreign*, or just not "what you like"? If you engaged in an act of sneaking last week, would you say you *sneaked* or *snuck*? And again, whichever one you "don't like," do you hear the other one as "not English"? Suffixes give you wiggle room.

But the other things, to people writing Old English, felt more disruptive. If the "right" way was *I **feared me of** financial ruin*, then *I feared financial ruin* was not just a matter of some little ending being different, but a whole different way of casting the sentence. This, like *Did you see what he's doing?*, was the kind of thing that would make it onto the page only at the dawn of a new day.

The scholars who are even skeptical that the Vikings were responsible for suffix decay miss this crucial difference between scripture and writing. In a classic monograph, two of them address "schwa drop." "Schwa" is the technical term for the muddy little sound in the *a* of *about* or the *o* in *lemon*. By "schwa drop" they refer to Old

English endings written as *-e* that were pronounced like the *a* in *about*, which in the Northumbrian dialect can be seen to disappear in documents closer to the Battle of Hastings. They note "Schwa drop occurred in the North long after Norse had died out there, so even though there is 'simplification' here, it can't be blamed on a language contact situation."

But yes, it can. These scholars are assuming that Anglo-Saxons lived in a world where things happening in every-day speech were immediately committed to the page. They neglect that even after Vikings' descendants were no longer speaking Old Norse, what a scribe would feel appropriate to engrave for posterity onto vellum with quill and ink would not be the "off" way that these Viking descendants were speaking English, whether or not they still spoke Old Norse. There would be something analogous to a seven-second delay.

Of course, we need not assume that the original Anglo-Saxon constructions were utterly dead as of Middle English. After all, the Vikings had occupied only half of the country. Rather, as often as not, the Viking impact rendered things that had once been *required* into things that were just *optional*, after which there was a snowball effect.

For example, when Jane Austen uses *be*-perfects that sound weird to us now—*I am so glad we are got acquainted*—we certainly will not assume that she was genuflecting to

Beowulf. She really talked that way. But the key point is that in all the other Germanic languages but one, as Austen wrote, the *be*-perfect was much more vital than it was in her English, and in those languages it lives today, going nowhere. Why, in Austen's time, was it on the ropes at all in English, while thriving elsewhere in Germanic and beyond? French and Italian show no signs of letting it randomly "disappear." The Viking impact—i.e., what distinguishes English from the other Germanic languages as well as French and Italian—got the dissolution started.

Monopoly Versus Clue

To traditional History of English scholars, my claim about what the Vikings did may seem hasty. But as with the Celtic issue, this is largely a matter of what we see as proof.

When it comes to charting how English got to be the way it is now from what it was in *Beowulf*, the common consensus is all about *describing* rather than *explaining*. "The such-and-such suffix *-en* eroded into *-uh*, then x centuries later it is gone entirely except in this document, likely written in a conservative register due to influence from factor y; meanwhile *-um* eroded into *-en*; see in Figure 7 how the erosion took place at such-and-such a rate in documents from this region but more slowly in documents from that region . . ."

That is, this kind of work shows us what happened

decade by decade in the English *scriptures*. Treating *scripture* as the only valid or interesting evidence in studying how English changed in ancient centuries risks leaving untold forever an interesting chapter in the saga of English. This is especially unsavory in that treating the peculiarity of Modern English as a matter of chance is like walking past cars parked along a street and happening upon one with the windshield broken in, three hubcaps gone, and no license plates, and deciding that all of this must have happened via ordinary wear and tear.

Maybe lightning did in the windshield. The hubcaps could have fallen off of their own accord and been picked up by trash collectors. But what about the other cars sitting intact? Okay, one car up the street is missing *one* hubcap. Another one has a hairline crack in its back window. But obviously, someone broke into this particularly smashed-up car. Something happened to it. Attention must be paid. We should report this car. Especially since this happens to be a neighborhood well known as a favored haunt of—oh, let's just toss the analogy and say *Vikings*!

Those who are uninterested in reporting this car are playing Monopoly, while those who are interested in reporting the attack on it are the ones bringing in a game of Clue and finding little interest. The Monopoly players like Monopoly; Clue just doesn't happen to be their bag. But as with the Celtic case, the Clue players happen to be in a better position to identify the truth than the ones enjoying Monopoly.

The Monopoly players are, to bring back the car analogy, like municipal photographers assigned to make snapshots of each street in the city every five years. They have no way of explaining why this particular car is so banged up, and really, they don't care. They have done their job to depict this car's state from one moment to the next and that's all. Photographers document—but historians explain.

English's simplicity is, in terms of explanation rather than mere documentation, weird. It is evidence of a blindsiding by adults too old to just pick up English thoroughly the way children of immigrants do. The Scandinavian Vikings left more than a bunch of words in English. They also made it an easier language. In this, in a sense, they clipped Anglophones' wings. The Viking impact, stripping English of gender and freeing us of attending to so much else that other Germanic speakers genuflect to in every conversation, made it harder for us to master other European languages.

To wit: so many people spoke English the way a lot of us speak French and Spanish that "off" English became the seedbed for literary English. I'm writing in it now. We speak not only a bastard tongue, but one with roots in its own mangling. English is interesting in much more than which words we use.

And knowing that, we are in a position to understand why it isn't true that, as we are often told, our grammar indicates what kind of people we are. To be a modern Anglophone is not to be a psychologically abbreviated version of an Anglo-Saxon villager. If you doubt that anyone has ever implied such, read on.

Four

DOES OUR GRAMMAR
CHANNEL OUR THOUGHT?

HINT: DOES ENGLISH GRAMMAR
CHANNEL YOURS?

To understand that English has developed not just via new words but also through the emergence of new grammar puts in a new light a notion about language you may have heard about.

One of the most popular ideas is that a language's grammar and the way its words pattern reflect aspects of its speakers' culture and the way they think. Countless times I have witnessed the hush in a classroom when introducing undergraduates to this hypothesis. If one doesn't pick this up in college, one will catch it in newspaper and magazine articles about indigenous groups, or even in bits of folk wisdom floating around. One sometimes hears that Iran is home to a uniquely vigorous homosexual subculture because its third person pronoun is the same for men and women.

This idea that grammar is thought became influential from the writings of Edward Sapir. We met him in the previous chapter venturing that English speakers came to find nuance irritating. Even that point had hints of the language-is-thought persuasion—supposedly the erosion of various aspects of English grammar was due to some psychological leaning in its speakers. But Sapir ventured only passing speculations in this vein.

It was Sapir's student Benjamin Lee Whorf who picked up the ball and ran with it, in the 1930s, publishing several pieces on the subject which served as its foundational texts. The hypothesis is known, therefore, as the Sapir-Whorf hypothesis.

The hypothesis has also failed. Repeatedly and conclusively.[1]

Decade after decade, no one has turned up anything showing that grammar marches with culture and thought in the way that the Sapir-Whorf hypothesis claimed. At best, there are some shards of evidence that language affects thought patterns in subtle ways, which do not remotely approach the claims of Whorf.

---

1. A useful summary of the record of this hypotheses from its inception up to the eighties is John A. Lucy, *Language Diversity and Thought: A Reformulation of the Linguistic Relativity Hypothesis* (Cambridge: Cambridge University Press, 1992). It should be noted that since then, there has been work faintly favorable to the hypothesis, albeit in no way bearing it out as proposed by Whorf and his followers. This has included work by Lucy, as well as work by scholars such as Paul Kay, Lera Boroditzky, and Daniel Colasanto.

Yet the Sapir-Whorf idea is cited enthusiastically in textbooks even today, and is a favorite approach to language by journalists. In 2004 a *New York Times* writer supposed that the language of the Kawesqar tribe in Chile has no future tense marking because, having been nomads traveling often in canoes in the past, they would usually have been so unclear on what was going to happen in the future that there was no need to ever talk about it (!). Never mind that Japanese has no future markers either, and yet the Japanese hardly seem unconcerned with the future. The point is that this *Times* writer would not have even floated such a notion if it weren't for the seed planted by Whorf's work seven decades previously. Whorf, even though he died in 1941, lent us a meme.

However, with an awareness of how languages actually come to be the way they are, we are in a position to truly understand how hopeless the Sapir-Whorf hypothesis is. The idea that our take on the world is mediated by refraction through our grammar, such that the world's six thousand languages generate six thousand correspondent world views, is deeply appealing. It is also mistaken.

A School Is Founded

After all, is the way I think shared with all of the other Anglophones of the world—or even just all Americans—and reflected in the language I am writing in right now?

Was the change from Old English *grammar* to Modern English *grammar*—not vocabulary—determined or even partially affected by the transformation of England from feudalism to industrial capitalism?

The answers to both questions would have to be yes, from the way Whorf wrote. His pièce de résistance was an observation about the language of the Hopi: that it does not mark time in any way. He argued that this made Hopi speakers think in a way completely different from us Westerners, with our persnickety obsession with past, present, and future. The Hopis, he argued, think of time as cyclical, to the extent that they even have a concept of "time" as an ongoing process in the way that we do.

Grammars do differ in what concepts they choose to mark. Spanish marks gender on nouns. Japanese does not, but it has markers showing whether a noun is a subject or object. All grammars mark some things; no grammar marks everything. Whorf's idea was that which things a grammar happens to mark determines what its speakers perceive most readily in their daily lives:

> Users of markedly different grammars are pointed by the grammars toward different types of observations and different evaluations of externally similar acts of observation, and hence are not equivalent as observers but must arrive at somewhat different views of the world.

Whorf, like many of his followers, was not quite clear as to whether he thought that grammar, once accidentally morphing into certain patterns, channeled culture, or that culture determined how grammar morphed. Presumably, there was a "dynamic" two-way relationship. But his basic point was the correspondence between grammar and thought patterns, and hence culture.

Therefore, Western scientific advances presumably correspond to our languages' rich tense marking: "Newtonian space, time, and matter are no intuitions. They are recepts from culture and language. That is where Newton got them." This is why, therefore, it was not Native Americans who gave the world theoretical physics.

Whorf, as it happened, was a fire insurance inspector by day, and perhaps it was partly because of this that he did not know Hopi very well. Quite simply, Hopi has as much equipment for placing events in time as any language. Here is *Start sharpening your arrows; we're going hunting*:

*Um **angwu**   **pay**   ùuhoy   tsuku-toyna-**ni**;*
you **beforehand already** your arrow make-a-point-**will**

*itam maq-to-**ni**.*
we   hunt-go-**will**

Hopi renders the statement as something like *You'll have sharpened your arrows, then we will go hunting*. And in doing so, we see two indications of pastness, and a thoroughly typical future marker. Hopi does not render the sentence as something like *Sharpen your arrows, as our hunting occurs in the cycle of time*. Yet Whorf's claim about Hopi was quite explicit; i.e., that Hopi has "no words, grammatical forms, constructions, or expressions that refer directly to what we call 'time,' or to past, or future, or to enduring or lasting."

In other words, Whorf was just wrong—and yet without the zest of his writings on Hopi, it is likely that the Sapir-Whorf hypothesis would not have caught on at all.

Of course, Whorf hedged a bit, admitting that grammar did not utterly prevent a person from being able to think about or talk about things the grammar did not explicitly mark. Rather, a grammar makes it much *easier* to think of and talk about some things than others:

> The potential range of perception and thought is probably pretty much the same for all men. However, we would be immobilized if we tried to notice, report, and think of all possible discriminations in experience at each moment of our lives. Most of the time we rely on the discriminations to which our language is geared, on what Sapir termed "grooves of habitual expression."

But the general tenor of Whorf's writings reveals little interest in the potential and an ardently promulgated obsession with the habitual:

> We cut nature up, organize it into concepts, and ascribe significances as we do, largely because we are parties to an agreement to organize it in this way— an agreement that holds throughout our speech community and is codified in the patterns of our language. The agreement is, of course, an implicit and unstated one, *but its terms are absolutely obligatory;* we cannot talk at all except by subscribing to the organization and classification of data which the agreement decrees.

The emphasis above is Whorf's, and his writing is sometimes almost narcoticized with his fascination with the exotic inner world of the Hopi as channeled through their purportedly tenseless tongue:

> It might be said that the linguistic background of Hopi thought equips it to recognize naturally that force manifests not as motion or velocity, but as cumulation or acceleration. Our linguistic background tends to hinder us in this same recognition, for having legitimately conceived

force to be that which produces change, we then think of change by our linguistic metaphorical analog, motion, instead of by a pure motionless changingness concept, i.e. accumulation or acceleration.

It isn't hard to see why so many smart people from the thirties on have thrilled to this notion, especially couched in such eloquent phrasing. Whorf was also a mesmerizing speaker, and a looker to boot. Yet because the foundational presentation was founded on sand and no one has since found any further confirmation elsewhere, it is dismaying to see how deeply the idea has permeated educated thought nevertheless.

Are We Dumb Anglo-Saxons?

Try squaring the Sapir-Whorf hypothesis with, for example, the fact that today's English was once Old English. As we have seen, the language I am writing in was not planted in one fell swoop from on high. Modern English is the current stage of what began as a very different grammar, much like German's. Over a millennium-and-a-half, this grammar had grammatical features from Celtic plugged into it Botox-style, while also being radically shorn of its complexities liposuction-style by adults learning it as a second language.

Now, let's try to look at this language we speak as it is today through the eyes of the Sapir-Whorf hypothesis. We English speakers "cut nature up, organize it into concepts, and ascribe significances as we do, largely because we are parties to an agreement to organize it in this way" and "cannot talk at all except by subscribing to the organization and classification of data which the agreement decrees." Or, as an early Whorfian put it:

> The thought of the individual must run along its grooves; but these grooves, themselves, are a heritage from individuals who laid them down in an unconscious effort to express their attitude toward the world. Grammar contains in crystallized form the accumulated and accumulating experience, the Weltanschauung of a people.

The problem is that according to this logic, the differences between Old English and Modern English grammar must reflect differences between Anglo-Saxon culture and life in modern New York or London.

So first of all, we now have meaningless *do*. Unlike Old English speakers, we have to say *I do not walk* and *Do I walk?* Thus, presumably, since Anglo-Saxon days, English speakers have become especially alert to negativity and uncertainty, such that we have to stress verbs with *do* in the relevant types of sentence. Obviously that makes no sense—it's simply that we snapped up meaningless *do* from Welsh and Cornish because speakers of those languages were learning English.

Now, as it happens, Whorf was not unaware that languages are always picking things up from one another, noting, "It is clear that linguistic determinism and linguistic relativity cannot be absolute in the face of the known facts of linguistic change, multilingualism, and cultural diffusion."

But even then, note what he wrote next: "People do make new discriminations and find linguistic expressions for them, often by borrowing." It sounds as if Whorf thought that speakers of a language took in features from another language only if those features provided a way of expressing the "new discriminations" they had fallen into.

That is, meaningless *do* made its way into English because English speakers for some reason had become uniquely alert to negation and questionhood and were ripe for some nearby language to give them a way to vent this alertness? But what about how in South Africa, Xhosa and Zulu picked up click sounds from Khoisan languages? Was it because they had drifted into a latent desire to make such sounds and the Khoisan languages just happened to fulfill the need? Or was it because, well, the languages spoken next door happened to have clicks in them? Clearly, drifting into "new discriminations" is not a precondition for taking a feature from another language. The precondition is, simply, proximity.

And then, what about how English got easier over the centuries? According to the Sapir-Whorf hypothesis, compared to Old English speakers, Modern English speakers are dimwits.

Since we no longer classify our nouns by gender, we are less sensitive to masculinity and femininity as abstract concepts. This implies that the fashion in late-twentieth-century academia for treating gender as a societal construct had actually penetrated the world view of Joe Barstool (Tavernstool?) as early as A.D. 1200.

We are, apparently, less alert to the fact that anger, remembrance, error, fear, and shame are things that we ourselves feel. Old English speakers "feared themselves" when they felt afraid just as they behaved themselves. These days, apparently, there is always a part of an Anglophone that supposes that, just maybe, his feelings are experienced by someone else.

And then, never mind that when we see a car coming, the fact that it is moving *to* here (*hither*) rather than already *here* is less vivid to us than it was vivid to an Anglo-Saxon farmer that a carriage was coming toward him rather than resting in front of him. Old English "cut nature up" in a way that rendered those farmers more aware of movement than we must be, with our one-size-fits-all *here*, *there*, and *where*.

We are also less clear on the difference between the immediate context of people we are talking to in the moment and people in the abstract. The Old English speaker had the pronoun *man* (actually pronounced "mon" in the way that we today associate with Anglophone Caribbeans) to refer to an abstract "they"—***Man** says that the language is getting easier*—or "one"—***Man** speaks Old English here!* But even though the typical Old English speaker spent his life in a village whereas the typical Modern English speaker has read newspapers, traveled some, and today has broadband, the Old English speaker's grammar rendered him more cosmopolitan than we are, more aware of a world beyond his own head.

And forget our processing that when we *have e-mailed* something, an action has been performed while when we *have left*, a state has arisen in which we *are gone*. When using the perfect, Old English speakers used *be* instead of *have*, with a bunch of verbs that referred more to how things ended up than an event happening. Apparently to us today, "states, schmates"—everything is an action.

In the several-decades'-deep literature on the Sapir-Whorf hypothesis, I am aware of no address of what its implications would be for how a language has changed over time. This is a serious problem, because if there is anything really interesting to the hypothesis, then surely we seek meaningful correlations between the culture of Anglo-Saxons, who spoke a grammar like German's, and the culture of Modern English speakers, who speak a language a little like Welsh and a lot like nothing else.

I venture that no scholar will see it as promising to investigate whether Modern English speakers are psychologically less alert to the nuance of daily experience than Anglo-Saxon villagers. And to the extent that Whorfians object that it is a two-way street and culture can also affect grammar, we wonder what it was about England becoming a literate, industrialized society that would have encouraged a simpler grammar.

The disconnection between cultural development and grammar is also clear in that societies have turned upside down over time while the grammar stayed put. As psychologist Herbert Clark has put it, if the Sapir-Whorf hypothesis "has any force historically, we should find examples of beliefs failing to change over time because of the conventions that exist in the language. Such examples do not readily come to mind."

Right—take Russia. All would agree that certain changes have occurred in prevailing beliefs in that country over the past thousand years—from brute feudalism under the tsars to Communism to glasnost to the queer blend of democracy and dictatorship of today. Yet Russian grammar during that time has always been the marvelous nightmare that it is now. Russian has changed, to be sure, but without equivalents to the Celtic adoption and the Viking disruption, and nowhere near as dramatically as English—and in no ways that could be correlated with things Peter the Great, the Romanovs, or Lenin did.

Whorfianism as Zeitgeist: Thinking People's Street Myth

Whenever you read someone making reference to the Whorfian perspective on language, whoever the writer picked it up from has never had occasion to address just why Modern English speakers are not rather troglodytic creatures compared to Anglo-Saxon-speaking warriors.

In general, there is curiously little interest among people fascinated by the Whorfian paradigm in examining whether a given grammatical trait conditions a certain way of thinking not just in one language, but in other ones. As towering a mind as literary critic Edmund Wilson, for example, thought the reason Russians seemed unable to keep to a schedule was that Russian is a language where future tense is indicated largely via context— but then Japanese is like that, too, and the Japanese have never seemed to have any problem with schedules.

Journalist Mark Abley, engaging writer though he is, falls into this trap in his enthusiasm for Whorfianism. In French and many other Western European languages, there are two words for *know*: *savoir* means to know a fact; *connaître* means to know a person or to be familiar with something. Abley has it that:

> My language allows me, somewhat clumsily, to get the distinction across: on the one hand, factual knowledge; on the other, acquaintanceship and understanding. But to a French speaker, that distinction is central to how the mind interacts with the world.

Really? Is Abley really so sure that the difference between knowing the capital of Nebraska and knowing a friend is more immediate to Gérard Depardieu than to Judi Dench? It's a cute idea, yes—but does Abley actually have any grounds for supposing that it is true?

How does it sound when it's French that has one word where English has more, and when it isn't something as immediately evident as the European *know* verbs? In French, *sortir* means "go out," but also covers what English would express with *come out* (in the earthquake, *le tiroir est sorti de la commode*, "the drawer came out of the dresser"), *get out* (someone is in a hole and says, *"Sors-moi d'ici!"*

"Get me out of here!"), and *stick out* as in one's tongue (*"Sors la langue,"* "Stick out your tongue").

So—are we English speakers more attuned than French speakers to the difference between leaving home, something slipping out of place, being yanked out of a hole, and sticking out our tongues? I would venture that the answer is no. To be a reasoning representative of *Homo sapiens* is to understand those four processes as radically different, whether or not your language happens to have the same word for them. The same applies to how your language happens to mark knowing.

Abley also shows us that the Boro language of India has verbs with charmingly specific meanings. The implication is that to speak Boro is to be uniquely attuned to these highly particular concepts, such as:

egthu: when people getting to know one another
     start to establish a sense of comfort and
     connection
onsay: musky bodily odor, especially that emanating
     from the armpits, of a kind not ideal but vaguely
     pleasant
goblo: when a romantic pair have been estranged for
     a long period and decide to be together again
khonsay: to have sex for the first time with someone
     you are in a romantic relationship with

asusu: when a member of a couple stays always a
  vigilant foot or so away from the other member at
  a social occasion

Interesting that a culture would choose those highly
particular aspects of experience to assign words to. Or is
it?—I actually dissembled there. The language with words
for those concepts is good old English; namely, *bonding,
funk, reconciliation, consummate,* and *hover.*

Upon which now we can take a look at what the Boro
words actually mean:

egthu: to create a pinching sensation in the armpit
khonsay: to pick an object up with care as it is rare or
  scarce
onsay: to pretend to love
goblo: to be fat (as a child or infant)
asusu: to feel unknown and uneasy in a new place

Abley's idea is that to speak Boro is to be uniquely
attuned to these concepts. However, when speakers of
a language are asked what a word means, quite often
they give particular uses that happen to be especially
common, rather than the larger concept the word technically covers. For example, if someone asked you what *consummate* meant, you would likely give the sexual meaning,

although you technically know that *consummate* means, more generally, "to bring to the highest level." "What's bonding?" someone asks you. You might say "When things stick together." But you also might say "When you first feel a click with someone, like guys bonding over sports."

This is surely a lot of what is behind the Boro verbs. After all, English has ways of expressing many of those concepts. "To create a pinching sensation in the armpit" can be expressed in English as *cinch* up into—and is *egthu* in Boro used exclusively with armpits, or was that what the consulted speaker most readily mentioned? To pick an object up with care in English can be to *pluck* it out. We have no verb for "to be fat as a child" but we have a noun, *baby fat,* which refers to exactly what the Boro word does, except not as a verb. The issue is not what part of speech people happen to express a concept in, but whether their language "feels" it. Well, on babies' fat, English feels it, as do quite certainly all languages on earth.

In the same way, we have no verb like *asusu* for not feeling at home, but we have positive adjectives like *acclimated* and *situated—I wasn't situated yet and so I was still calling home every night.* English speakers are attuned to the same mental state that Boro speakers are when they *asusu.*

And even where Boro really does have a word marking a fine shade of human experience that English does not— I draw a blank on an English equivalent to "pretend to love"—it still doesn't follow that this experience is more deeply felt by them than the rest of us.

Looking at our own language is an especially effective way of truly getting this. In English, something in spot four is *fourth,* in spot seven is *seventh,* in spot eight is *eighth,* and so on. Only the first three numbers are distorted in a major way: *first* and *second* don't correspond to *one* and *two* at all, and *third* clearly has *three* in there, but beaten up a bit, and what's with the *-rd*? There's no *sixrd* or *tenrd.*

Well, that's something else weird about English and European languages. Most of the world's languages have a special word for the first spot, like *first,* but then just say, as it were, "two-th," "three-th." So English's *second,* Spanish's *segundo,* and Russian's *vtoroj* (when *two* is *dva*) mean that these languages channel our European language speakers' thoughts into a heightened awareness of sec-ondness, I suppose. That is, an English, Spanish, or Russian speaker is more sensitive to things being second than a German, a Turk, an Inuit, or an Israeli . . . Come on. We just happen to have a distinct word marking sec-ondness; the Boro just happen to have a word for pre-tending to love.

Politics or Science?

Among academics and beyond, the Sapir-Whorf hy-pothesis has been, quite commonly, less examined than embraced. One of the reasons: what interests many about the hypothesis is less what it would imply for academic issues about human psychology than its demonstration that indigenous cultures are not "primitive," and in fact may have some things on us.

This was an explicit mission of Sapir, and an invaluable one in itself. It is to him and like-minded thinkers of his time such as his mentor anthropologist Franz Boas that it is part of the warp and woof of modern Westerners to view other cultures as variations on being human rather than "savages." Gone are the days when America could stampede into the Philippines as it did during the McKinley administration, casually assuming that the "natives" needed to be "civilized."

Whorf inherited the diversity imperative from Sapir, and it permeates his writings on Hopi. To Whorf, Hopi and the world view it supposedly conditioned was not just different, but better:

> Does the Hopi language show here a higher plane of thinking, a more rational analysis of situations, than our vaunted English? Of course it does. In this field and in various others, English compared to Hopi is like a bludgeon compared to a rapier.

We Westerners are obsessed with putting things into little boxes, drawing boundaries—the Hopi, however, are more in touch with higher realities:

Our objectified view of time is, however, favorable
to historicity and to everything connected with
the keeping of records, while the Hopi view is
unfavorable thereto. The latter is too subtle, complex,
and ever-developing, supplying no ready-made
answer to the question of when "one" event ends
and "another" begins.

The problem with this kind of thing is that too often
it ends up, in essence, taking us back to the noble savage.
Noble, to be sure, but in what we celebrate in them as
special, savage—clothed chimpanzees, cute.

Mark Abley, for instance, seizes upon a grammatical
quirk in the Native American languages of the Algonquian family, such as Cree, Ojibwa, and the Powhatan
that Pocahontas spoke. In one of them, Montagnais, the
way you say *You see me* is:

Tshi - ua:pam - in.
you   see   me

But the way to say *I see you* is not to put *I* before the
verb and *you* after. That is, reversing the example above
and doing

In - ua:pam - tshi.
I   see   you

is wrong; it is not Montagnais at all, any more than
Reading book you a are is English.

Instead, you use the *You see me* sentence, but stick a
little syllable into it to make it mean *I see you*:

Tshi - ua:pam - in.
you   see   me

*Tshi - ua:pam - **it** - in.*
you   see   me = "I see you."

So—the basic sentence is about *you*; only with an ad-
justment can you make it about *I*. (That is, indeed, so de-
liciously odd from our Anglophone perspective. Once
again, languages are interesting in their *grammars* as well
as their words.)

Abley has it that this means that Algonquian language
speakers are less self-centered than Europeans, and that
"to speak properly, in an Algonquian language, is to be
aware of the identities and interrelationships of all the
people you address." But when we are at a Thanksgiving
dinner, are we English speakers not fully aware of who is
who, despite that we can put *I* first?

Abley marvels at the fact that Native Americans are
capable of carrying on conversations among multiple
participants—which is like praising a culture for cooking

food or, really, being more cognitively advanced than their pets.

And in any case, just as Whorf mischaracterized Hopi, Abley leaves out that in Algonquian languages, *I* can indeed come first. *You*, if there, does have to come first, but if there is no *you* around and the *I* is interacting with a *he*, *she*, *it*, or *they*, then *I* has to come first. In another Algonquian language, Cree, *I frighten them* is:

Ni - se:kih - a - wak.
I   frighten   them

To say *They frighten me* you can't put *they* first; you make *they* the subject by sticking in a special syllable:

*Ni - se:kih -   **ik** - wak*
I   frighten   them = "They frighten me."

It looks like Algonquians are just as narcissistic as we are when *I* am talking about *them*.

One episode that pointed up this fundamental commitment to ennobling The Other was the rare language-is-thought study that argued that English speakers are the more insightful ones. Alfred Bloom noted that in Chinese, one must engage in a certain amount of circumlocution to be explicit that something is hypothetical rather than real. In English we can say *If you saw my sister, you would know that she was pregnant.* But in Chinese, the sentence is rendered as "If you see my sister, you know she is pregnant." For those who know Mandarin:

Rúguǒ nǐ   kàn dào   wo mèimei
if   you see arrive I   sister

nǐ   yídìng   zhīdào tā   huáiyùn   le.
you certainly know   she pregnant now

That sentence can have various meanings. One of them is neutral and not hypothetical:

"If you see my sister, you'll know she is pregnant."

Then there are hypothetical meanings, referring to something that has not happened or did not happen:

"If you saw my sister, you'd know she was pregnant."
"If you had seen my sister, you'd have known she was pregnant."

In Mandarin, context determines which meaning comes through.

Bloom did an experiment that showed Chinese speakers less alert to hypotheticality when reading stories in Chinese than English speakers reading the stories in English. On the basis of this, he supposed that since where people's grammar is concerned, "the thought of the individual must run along its grooves" as the Whorfian I quoted above had it, Mandarin's grooves must distract thought from the difference between reality and the hypothetical. What's good for a perceptively challenged Modern English speaker is good for the man on the street in Beijing, right?

Apparently not: people shot at Bloom like he was a varmint. Their objections to details of his experimental procedure were reasonable, but more conclusive was their insistence that Chinese speakers process hypotheticality via context even if their grammar does not mark it as explicitly as English's. Elsewhere, however, there is little interest in noting that, say, English speakers understand via context that *knowing* algebra is different from *knowing* the man next door, or that even if Hopi did have no tense markers, we could assume that its speakers processed that things happen before and after one another as vividly as we do. I feel reasonably confident in surmising that if Bloom's study had shown some interpretational deficit among English speakers, no one would have batted an eye.

A speaker of American Sign Language captured the essence of how Whorfianism unintentionally demeans minority languages, mocking outsider fans of Sign. In an interview, the signer feigned "a vapid, rapt look on his face. 'Sign language is so *beautiful*,' he signs, in a gushing mockery of the attitude that exoticizes sign and correspondingly reduces deaf people to the status of pets, mascots. 'It's just so *wonderful* that deaf people can *communicate!*'" Or, I would have it, "It's just so *wonderful* that people who aren't like us can *think* and *process reality* as richly as we do!"

Maybe that message had a certain value in Whorf's era. In the thirties, popular culture and common consensus in America were still shot through with pitiless condescension toward "natives," "Chinks," "jungle bunnies." But it's been a while. We clap when our infants don't spill their food. We can afford to let go of clapping when exotic folks don't, when in our times, celebrating diversity is a shibboleth of moral legitimacy among thinking First World people, and considerably, if not comprehensively, beyond.

All *Homo sapiens* engage in advanced mentation—yes, hallelujah. However, this doesn't make the Cree speaker a paragon of enlightened selflessness because *you* comes earlier than *I* in his way of saying *I see you*, any more than our ability to explicitly get across *If you'd have seen my sister, you'd have known she was pregnant* makes us Anglophones wizards of truth versus falsity compared to people in China.

Does Language Channel Thought?:
The Neo-Whorfians

At this point, one might ask: does language channel thought at all? It is pretty clear that people speaking non-Western languages are not walking around in psychedelic dreamscapes channeling essences of The Real unknown to us "straights" marching around in business suits. However, is it really true that grammar has *nothing* to do with the way we think?

Of course not. These days there is research being done in what is often called the Neo-Whorfian School. No more of the mystic, anti-Western hocus-pocus—this is serious psychological research, based on a reasoned curiosity as to whether grammar can channel thought, albeit in ways less dramatic than the straight-up Whorfians were seeking. And there are, indeed, twinkles of evidence in favor of the Sapir-Whorf hypothesis. Nothing mind-bending or kaleidoscopic—just twinkles.

In some cases, there is a chicken-and-egg issue that makes it hard to see the study as telling us that language channels culture rather than vice versa. The Guugu Yimithirr of Australia do not have terms like *in front of*. Instead, they refer to everything according to points on the compass—to the north of, to the south of—regardless of where they are in relation to the object. If a tree is in front of them, but in the global sense, it is to the south of them, they refer to it as south of them.

Neat—but is it that their language just happened not to have terms like *in front of* and *behind* and forced them to think of things in terms of compass points, or that their culture happened to focus on compass points and that determined how their language described position? Because the focus on compass points is so clearly a cultural peculiarity compared to most people on earth, it is hard to see from this experiment why grammar is a more likely explanation. More to the point, it isn't really surprising that people do not have terms for something their culture does not care about—i.e., that observation would not have sparked a whole school of thought the way Whorf's did.

In the same way, the Pirahã tribe of the Amazon have attracted media attention as a people whose language has no words for colors, numbers, or quantification (e.g., *all*, *every*), and does not even have relative or subordinate clauses—for *That's the guy who built my house* one can only say *That guy—he built my house*. The Pirahã prove incapable of performing even elementary mathematical tasks, and the media first jumped on this, predictably, as proof of the old-fashioned language-makes-thought notion: because the Pirahã language has no numbers, the people are rendered incapable of doing math. Again, however, this puts the cart before the horse. The Pirahã are hunter-gatherers who subsist on their own. Their lives therefore afford them no reason to manipulate precise numerical concepts, such as for trade or constructing elaborate architectural monuments. In addition, the Pirahã are an unusually incurious people (no, really, they are—consult the source in the Notes on Sources), which makes them especially uninterested in fine-grained manipulation of numerals.

A natural outcome, then, would be that their language would have no words for numbers. The magical idea that language is the issue—i.e., that they would be doing algebra if only it weren't for the mysterious happenstance that their language has no numbers—may have more visceral oomph, but little else. The Pirahã's chronicler, Dan Everett, concurs, despite the media's occasionally making it seem otherwise—it's what the Pirahã are like that shapes what their language is like, not the other way around. I'm not sure how truly interesting that, in itself, is, despite how interesting the Pirahã are themselves, as well as their language—albeit for reasons other than their grammar purportedly channeling its speakers' thought patterns.

More interesting are cases where culture cannot possibly be the issue. In German, the word for *key* is masculine (*der Schlüssel*). If you give the key a personal name, Germans tend to have an easier time recalling it if the name is masculine; they more readily associate the key with a picture of a man than a woman, and describe it with words like *hard, heavy, jagged, metal, serrated,* and *useful.* In Spanish, the word for *key* is feminine (*la llave*), and Spanish speakers are more comfortable with keys' having female names, associating them with pictures of women, and they tend to describe them as *golden, intricate, little, lovely, shiny* and *tiny.* Maybe it is relevant that when I once asked a Dutch person what keys were like (*key* in Dutch is the masculine *sleutel*), she said, with a distinct animation, "I imagine a big, giant key with decorations on it like the kind that would open a castle!!" I don't know why she pictured that precisely, but I take the liberty of assuming that the key she imagined was a fella.

So speakers of languages with gender, deep down inside, have a sense that objects are boys and girls. It is also documented that a Spanish speaker, if asked to imagine a table (*la mesa*) as a talking cartoon character, is likely to imagine the table's voice being high and sweet because in their language *table* is feminine.

However, in real life it is very, very rare that we go about imagining inanimate objects talking at all. In general, speakers of languages that assign gender to nouns do not on an everyday basis see inanimate objects as sexed "men" and "women." The gender class of objects is something lying deep in their psyches, which we can tease out with careful experiments. However, it has nothing to do with the immediacy of daily experience. For anyone who has been close to a speaker of a language with gender, think about it—do they give any evidence of thinking of chairs and toothbrushes as "God's creatures," with a sex and the traits traditionally associated with it?

Unless you have known some truly unusual people (likely fond of dropping acid), you will agree that the gender that their native grammar happens to assign to in-animate objects does not color their world view. If it does, it is in a way that would seem significant only to an aca-demic psychologist plumbing exquisitely fine-grained niceties, hard to classify as a "world view" that would in-terest even the educated layman.

Studies like this show that language does have some glimmers of effect on thought. But they do not support the more dramatic implications that suck the air out of a room when the textbook version of Sapir-Whorf is brought up. They bring to mind University of California linguist Paul Kay's pithy observation about the whole business: "If anthropologists had not assumed that the people they went out to study have 'world views,' would they have found them?" Neo-Whorfians reveal the truth: perceptual distinctions of a subtle, slight, and subconscious nature, not "world views."

There is nothing "cultural" about imagining dulcet-toned tables if forced to by someone supervising an experiment you signed up for, with said experiment being the only time in your life when you will ever imagine a table with the power of speech. Paul Kay and Willett Kempton, who have done research in the Neo-Whorfian tradition, readily acknowledge the simple truth: "If the differences in world view," they write, "are to be interesting, they must be sizable. Minuscule differences are dull."

And yet, mainstream sources continue to flag the Sapir-Whorf hypothesis in its grand old rendition as a going concern. "The significance of Whorf's hypothesis lies less in its possible truth, and more in its continuing ability to generate thought and discussion on a problem which is central to the whole anthropological project," Alan Barnard and Jonathan Spencer have it in the *Encyclopedia of Social and Cultural Anthropology*. Or, as a widely used college textbook casually recites: "The Sapir-Whorf hypothesis therefore might suggest that English speakers can't help paying more attention to differences between males and females than do the Palaung and less than do French or Spanish speakers."

But again, what is the value of an investigation classified as ever "might suggesting," which inherently includes a hypothesis that Modern English is a philistine grammar, numb to the details that Old English channeled its speakers into noticing every day, such as the personal nature of emotion, or whether things are approaching us or sitting still?

The idea that the world's six thousand languages condition six thousand different pairs of cultural glasses simply does not hold water. The truly enlightened position is that, by and large, all humans, be they Australian Aborigines, Japanese urbanites, Kalahari hunter-gatherers, Cree Indians, Serbs, Greeks, Turks, Uzbeks, Amazonians, or Manhattanites in analysis, experience life via the mental equipment shared by all members of our species. No one is "primitive," but just as important, no one is privileged over others with a primal connection to The Real.

Five

SKELETONS IN THE CLOSET

WHAT HAPPENED TO ENGLISH
BEFORE IT WAS ENGLISH?

The final chapter in our new History of English takes us back before English was even English. It's a trip we need to take, because it reinforces two lessons I have tried to get across in this book. First, there is nothing unique about English's "openness" to words from other languages. Second, there is no logical conception of "proper" grammar as distinct from "bad" grammar that people lapse into out of ignorance or laziness.

We're going to go back before Old English, to Proto-Germanic, the ancestor to English and the other Germanic languages. It would appear that long before Something Happened to English, Something Happened to Proto-Germanic as well. There was a history of bastardy in English long before it was even a twinkle in Proto-Germanic's eye.

Froto- (I mean, Proto-) Germanic Sounded Strange

As I noted earlier, Proto-Germanic was never written, but we can hypothesize what its words—and also a lot of its grammar—were like by deduction from its modern descendants. Proto-Germanic was one of several branches of an even earlier language linguists call Proto-Indo-European, which was reconstructed in the same way, by comparing all of its branches. As it happens, Proto-Germanic was a distinctly weird offshoot of Proto-Indo-European. There was something not quite right about it.

For one thing, something had happened to its consonants. Where Proto-Indo-European words began with *p, t,* and *k,* for some reason in Proto-Germanic, they began with *f, th,* and *h,* respectively. We know this because only in Germanic languages today do the words come out that way, whereas in normal Indo-European languages they still have *p, t,* and *k.* Where Latin has *pater,* English has *father*—just as German has *Vater,* with the *v* pronounced "f," etc. Why? Where Latin has *tres,* English has *three.* Why? Where Latin has *canis,* English has *hound.* Why?

There are some sound changes that are so common you can almost guarantee that they will happen sooner or later in any language. For example, the standard Italian *cappicola* has morphed in Sicilian Italian to sound like this: "gabagul." The *g* sound is a version of the *k* sound of the *c*'s in *cappicola*—say *g* and *k* to yourself and see how similar they are. In the same way, the *b* sound in the middle of "gabagul" is a version of the *p* sound. So *k* sounds become *g* sounds all the time, as do *p* sounds become *b* ones. It's also typical for vowel sounds that carry no accent to drop off over time, such that "gabagul" doesn't have the old -*a* on the end of *cappicola*.

But *p* to *f*? Imagine a generation starting to say "fopcorn" instead of *popcorn*—weird. And even *t* to *th*: we pronounce the *t* in *water* more like a *d* because *d* is similar to *t* (try it). But it's hard to imagine someone saying "thop" instead of *top*. Yet this is what happened in Proto-Germanic, and it passed down into all of today's Germanic brood. As the way sounds change over time goes, *k* morphing into *h* is not all that odd, but *p* morphing into *f* and *t* morphing to *th* are not things your typical Indo-European language pulls. They aren't utterly unheard-of: worldwide, for example, *p*'s becoming *f*'s is not something a linguist is flabbergasted by, any more than it is mesmerizingly counterintuitive that Americans make lemonade while Finns don't (and they don't—it's weird; I couldn't find any during six weeks in Helsinki). But *p* becoming *f* wasn't the fashion within the Indo-European family. Why did the Germanic branch go its own way?

The process by which Proto-Indo-European sounds regularly changed into these other ones was discovered, as it happens, by one of the Grimm brothers famous for collecting and penning fairy tales (Jacob), and is known to linguists as Grimm's Law. Beyond our little circle, it should just be known as something weird about Germanic consonants.

Now, as always, there are some people inclined to assume this was just an accident. Then, again as always, others seek an explanation, and those who do suppose that Proto-Germanic must represent a branch of Proto-Indo-European that was learned by speakers of some other language. Because foreigners typically render a second language with an accent—that is, they filter it partially through the sounds of their own language—we might have an explanation as to why *p*, *t*, and *k* were distorted so abruptly in Germanic while they weren't in the Slavic, Greek, Celtic, or so many other branches of Indo-European.

But what language would these foreigners have been speaking? Well, *f*, *th*, and *h* have something in common: all of them are "hissy" sounds. *P*, *t*, and *k* are clipped sounds, called *stops* by linguists (hissy sounds are *fricatives*). Crucially, Proto-Indo-European was quite poor in hissy sounds—all it had was *s*, which came out as *z* here and there. It would seem that whoever took up Proto-Germanic spoke a language with a lot of hiss in it.

Linguists and archaeologists assume that Proto-

Germanic was being spoken in the last several centuries B.C. If we look for a language family other than Indo-European that was being spoken in or around Europe at this time, it happens that the Semitic family of the Middle East had good hissy languages.

Today, Semitic's most prominent representatives are Arabic and Hebrew. In the last centuries B.C., however, these were both obscure languages of small groups, and the shop-window Semitic representatives, used as lingua francas in the Middle East and/or beyond, were other ones. Akkadian is often mentioned via the names of its dialects Assyrian and Babylonian. Aramaic was once so entrenched as the language of note in the Middle East and beyond that it was the language of administration under the Persian Empire, run in Persia vastly eastward of where Aramaic had arisen, despite the native language of Persia's rulers being, well, Persian, completely unrelated to Aramaic. It lives on today among small groups, termed, for one, Syriac. Akkadian had *z, s, sh, ts,* and an *h* sound that you made with your uvula. Aramaic at the time had *sh, dz, ts,* and *h*. Snaky sounds.

So, just hypothetically, if speakers of languages like these wrapped their tongues around Proto-Germanic, we might expect that their rendition would have more hissy sounds than Proto-Indo-European passed down to it. But this alone can be so compelling only as a speculation. For one thing, one other Indo-European branch went hissy, too, apparently all by itself: Armenian, which occupies its branch all alone. *Pater* (*father*) in Latin, *hayr* in Armenian. *Cor* (*heart*) in Latin, *sirt* in Armenian.

Proto-Germanic Had Strange Verbs

But there was something else about Proto-Germanic.

To an English speaker it feels pretty normal that as often as not, we put a verb into the past by changing the vowel in it instead of adding *-ed*: *see, saw; drink, drank; come, came*; etc. And in Germanic in general, it is indeed normal: in German, those verbs are *sehe, sah; trinke, trank; komme, kam*. But in Indo-European, beyond Germanic, this is not normal at all.

You may know this from taking French or Spanish: there are certainly irregular verbs, but the irregularity is only rarely just a matter of switching a vowel. In Spanish, you start with an innocent infinitive form like *tener* ("to have"), and then cut your teeth on mastering that *he has* is *él tiene* but *he had* is *él tuvo*. It's not just the *u* vowel—there is also that random *v* that comes out of nowhere. Typical—and not just a matter of vowel switches alone, like *come, came; drink, drank*. These, where it's all about the one vowel, are Germanic's kink. In all Germanic languages, there is a long list of verbs whose pasts are formed like this, traditionally termed "strong verbs."

The reason this is not the case in other Indo-European subfamilies is because Proto-Indo-European was not like this. Its grammar did involve switching vowels—but to do an array of things such as helping to indicate case: if you asked a Proto-Indo-European speaker what a dog was called, they would have said it was a *kwōn*, with a long *o*. But in the genitive it was *kun-és* with a *u*, and in the accusative, *kwón-m̥* with a short *o* instead of a long one. Indicating past tense was only one thing vowel switching was used for (*know*, *knew* was *wid*, *woid*)—and only so much. In other branches of Proto-Indo-European, this vowel-switching machinery was passed down in assorted renditions reflecting that array of functions it had in Proto-Indo-European. Only in Proto-Germanic did the all-over-the-place vowel-switching of Proto-Indo-European morph into something as distinct and particular as a long list of past tense verb forms indicated with a vowel change and just that.

Once again, Proto-Germanic is odd. That's in two ways now. Might there be a reason? Well, what about those Semitic languages again? Interesting—their kink is that they form the past tense by changing the vowels inside the word. In Hebrew today, *he writes: hu kotev*. But *he wrote: hu katav*. The consonants stay the same: the vowels change: *write*, *wrote*; *kotev*, *katav*. All Semitic languages have had this feature, ancient and modern, including good old Akkadian and Aramaic. Hmm.

Even these two things are not quite a smoking gun, but there's something else.

Proto-Germanic Packed Light

Amid early offshoots of Proto-Indo-European, Proto-Germanic was like English amid Germanic languages in how much frippery it had lost. Proto-Indo-European marked its nouns with eight cases. Latin, the early Indo-European language most learned in modern times, held on to six: nominative, genitive ("of the table"), dative ("to the table"), accusative (table as object), ablative ("by the table"), and vocative (if you were moved to say "Oh, table!!" but more usually, of course, with names), and then some words had a locative (*Romae*, "in Rome"). The ancestor of today's Slavic languages, Old Church Slavonic, had seven cases, as Lithuanian still does. Old Irish, an early Celtic language, had five, like Ancient Greek then and Albanian now.

But Proto-Germanic had just four. Those four cases in German wear out Anglophone learners today, but in the grand scheme of things, they are a broken-down half of what Proto-Indo-European had.

In the same way, as Indo-European languages go, it's weird that in English the only verb endings are ones for present and past tense. *I wait, I waited,* and that's about it. German, as busier as it seems to us Anglophones, is pretty much the same: *ich warte, ich wartete.* There are no endings that mark the future, for example: English does future with a word, *will*; German uses its *werden* in the same way. That's how it is in all Germanic languages; that's how it was in Proto-Germanic.

Note, however, that in Spanish, you use endings to mark not only the present (*yo hablo*) and past (*yo hablé*), but imperfect (*hablaba*), future (*hablaré*), conditional (*hablaría*), subjunctive (*hable*), and imperfect subjunctive (*hablase*). Spanish is not unique here, but normal: it has stayed like Proto-Indo-European was, in which there were separate tables of endings to place things in time according to very specific gradations almost imposingly baroque. In fact, Spanish has taken this even further than Proto-Indo-European did in some ways, sprouting its own new endings. Proto-Indo-European, for example, did not have conditional endings.

This anality about assembling sentences very precisely regarding time and hypotheticality with endings was already de rigueur way back when Spanish was Latin. While Latin was spoken, when Proto-Germanic endings were down to just marking whether something was happening now or already had, Latin endings were painting a much more particular picture of how one experienced actions in time: *portō* ("I carry"), *portābam* ("I was carrying"), *portāvi* ("I carried"), *portāveram* ("I had carried"), *portābo* ("I will carry"), *portāverō* ("I will have carried").

Where did all of this go in Proto-Germanic? Some

descendants of Proto-Indo-European have held on to more of this stuff than others, but in Proto-Germanic it fell away to a peculiar extent, such that we Germanic speakers have dragooned little words like *will* and *would* to pick up the slack.

After what we have seen in this book, the reader will intuit that this suggests that Proto-Germanic was not just bastardized by some other language, but beaten up by it. The streamlining of Proto-Germanic, with its four little cases, and suffixes marking just two little tenses, is the sign of busy adults making their way in the language as best they could but never quite mastering the subtleties. Proto-Germanic seems to have been a kind of schoolboy Proto-Indo-European.[1]

---

1. In fact, there was one other ancient Indo-European branch that was about as slim around the waist as Proto-Germanic. Hittite, a long-extinct language spoken in what is now Turkey, had two genders rather than the classic three that Proto-Indo-European is thought to have had, and less verb-marking equipment than a card-carrying early Indo-European language typically hefted around. However, many heavy-hitting scholars of Indo-European have long argued that Hittite was what Proto-Indo-European itself was like, and that languages like Latin came later. That is, at first Proto-Indo-European, a language about as elaborated as Hittite but nowhere near as elaborated as Latin, split into two languages. One was Hittite itself, or more properly, the small family of now extinct languages Hittite was a part of, called Anatolian. Hittite and company stayed like Proto-Indo-European, which would have had, for example, just two genders rather than three. Call that "Proto-Indo-European Number One" or PIE1. But then there was the other first branch of Proto-Indo-European, which we will call PIE2. PIE2 happened to sprout a bunch of new conjugations, and a new gender alongside the original two. This busy language then morphed into all of the modern Indo-European families, including Germanic. Among these families, if grammar were foliage, only Germanic proceeded to clip the hedges into bushes instead of letting them become trees. Thus Proto-Germanic remains the odd one out, having alone shed so much of what Hittite, albeit looking similar to it, cannot have shed since it never had it.

At this point, many will see it as at least worth asking: just who might these people stirring up Proto-Germanic have been?

Proto-Germanic Was Full of Orphan Words

A final and conclusive piece of evidence that there were, at the very least, some people of some kind stirring things up is that no less than a third of the Proto-Germanic vocabulary does not trace back to Proto-Indo-European.

With the other two-thirds, we can first figure out what the Proto-Germanic word was, like *daukhtrô* for *daughter*, and then we can compare that word to *daughter* words in the other Indo-European subfamilies, and work out that the Proto-Indo-European source root was *dhugəter*.

But with a mysterious many of the Proto-Germanic words, we just hit a wall. There are no cognates of these words in other Indo-European languages, and thus no ancestral Proto-Indo-European word can be reconstructed. Earlier than Proto-Germanic the trail runs cold. The words quite often refer to seafaring (*sea, ship, strand, sail*), warmaking (*sword*), fish (*carp, eel*), and formal social institutions (*knight*). Note, for example, that there is no word akin to *sea* in any other European language you might be familiar with. In Romance, it's words like French's *mer* and Italian's *mare*. In the Slavic languages, Russian has *more*, Polish *morze*. Over in Celtic, in Welsh the word is *môr*.

From the shape of all those words, it is no surprise that it is thought that in Proto-Indo-European there was a word *mere* that referred, at least, to something like a lake. But in English we instead have this *sea* thing, with cognates like German's *See* and Dutch's *zee*. Why don't we English speakers refer to eating something like "Mar-food" instead of *seafood*? Sure, Germans, for example, also have *Meer* as an alternate. But where did their *See* come from?

Now, one way of approaching this is to just treat it as an accident. Who knows, after all, whether in other Indo-European languages, words related to the seemingly orphan ones in Proto-Germanic were once alive, but happened to drop out of use by chance? Maybe it happened that a Proto-Indo-European root now survives only in one of the many branches of the family. Although we would have to wonder why it would have blown away in so many branches so uniformly—but still.

Or, the meanings of words can change so much over time that a Proto-Germanic word could possibly trace to a Proto-Indo-European root with a completely different meaning, such that no one would suspect the connection. The word *punch*, when referring to a drink, comes not from a Proto-Indo-European word for some kind of liquid, but from its word for *five*—through Hindi's *five* word, used because the original recipe was developed in India and used five ingredients. Shitte happens.

And besides, when scholars put their heads to it they

can often figure out a Proto-Indo-European root that the Proto-Germanic words could have come from, via likenesses that no one happened to notice before.

So one leading scholar of how languages change has only this to say about the issue in a recent work:

> Shifts in the meanings of words and the replacement of old lexemes by new ones are universal types of language change; it is therefore not surprising that the lexicon of PGmc [Proto-Germanic], like that of all language, included many words of doubtful or unknown origin (e.g. *blōþą* "blood," *bainą* "bone," *handuz* "hand," *regną* "rain," *stainaz* "stone," *gōdaz* "good," *drinkaną* "drink," etc).

Well, yes. But what about when the mysterious words look—mysteriously—like ones in other language families? Like, say, Semitic?

For example, one of those words that does not trace before Proto-Germanic is *fright*. Its spelling reflects that there was once an extra consonant sound before the final *t*, and its rendition in other Germanic languages often gives us a better sense of the original, such as German's *Furcht*, pronounced "foorkht." The extra consonant was the sound of *ch* in *Bach*: the Proto-Germanic form was *furkhtaz*.

But check this out. The Proto-Semitic verb for "to

fear," as it happens, had the consonants *p-r-kh*. I give no
vowels because Semitic verbs *are* their trios of consonants;
the vowels change to mark tense and other distinctions,
as in *kotev/katav* ("write/wrote") above, and there is no
"default" vowel pattern that means nothing and signifies
a "basic" form. Thus, the closest we can come to what
"the word" for *fear* in Proto-Semitic was is *p-r-kh*.

Now, we can compare *p-r-kh* with the consonants in
furkhtaz:

p—r—kh
f—r—kh—t

The *f* and the *p* don't look related at first, but then
remember that in Proto-Germanic, *p* got turned into
f! The *p-r-kh* root for "to fear" just might have also
ended up as the word *fright* in England, and hence, on
this page.

Or, *folk* started in Germanic as a word referring to a division of an army, and only later morphed into meaning
a tribe or a nation. The Proto-Germanic word was *fulka*;
the early Semitic root for *divide*—i.e., as in making a
division—was *p-l-kh*:

p—l—kh
f—l—k

In the early Semitic language Assyrian, that root was used to mean *district* (i.e., a division of land), with the *kh* softening into a *g* (*puluggu*). In Hebrew today, a detachment is a *plaga*. Maybe in Northern Europe, that root came out as *fulka* in the same meaning.

Maiden was, in Old English, *mægden* and *mægþ*. The same word in Old Scandinavian was *magað*, in Old High German *magad*, in Gothic *magaþs*. Based on them, a plausible Proto-Germanic form would be *magaþ*. To which we can compare what can be reconstructed as an early Semitic form, *makhat:*

Early Semitic	m	a	kh	a	t
Proto-Germanic	m	a	g	a	þ

As we saw with *puluggu* in Assyrian, *kh* easily becomes *g*. Then, the change from *t* to *th* is that Proto-Germanic kink again.

Of course one must be careful making too much of it when words with the same meaning have similar shapes in different languages. As often as not, it's just an accident: the word for "hang down" is *sagaru* in Japanese, but not because Germanic-speaking Vikings made a hitherto unrecorded swing over to Japan and married a bunch of the women!

But the Semitic parallels with the orphan Proto-

Germanic words get more interesting when it's relation-
ships between words that are paralleled as well. Biblical
Hebrew had a word ʕebɛr that meant "to cross," and the
three-consonant root was also used in the word for *shore*.
Interesting that in Old English, *ofer* was the word for
both *shore* and *over*, as in the direction one goes when
crossing.

ʕebɛr and *ofer* are more similar than they may seem at
first. The ʕ at the beginning of ʕebɛr was something we
can treat as trivial, a sound produced back in the throat,
similar to the one we would make if we were talking about
apples and someone insisted on thinking we were talking
about pears, and we said, "I'm not talking about pears.
I'm talking about apples. *Apples,* damn you—*apples*!!!!"
Note that especially on that final utterance of apples, you
would begin the word not with the *a* vowel itself, but with
a catch in the throat, just like you utter at the start of both
syllables in "uh-oh!" The ʕ sound is just farther back in
the throat, but for our purposes we can imagine the Biblical Hebrew word as *"ebɛr"* just as English has no "letter"
for the catch in the throat before the two syllables in
"uh-oh!"

And then, the ḇ sound in Hebrew was rather like
blowing—the *v*-inflected *b* sound that you often learn in
Spanish classes—which was quite similar to the *f* in *ofer*.
German even maintains the connection between *shore*
and *over*: *shore* is *Ufer*, while *over* is *über*.

Another one: normally, Indo-European languages' word for *seven* has a *t* in it. French's *sept*, Spanish's *siete*, Greek's *heptá*, Polish's *siedem* (note that in your mouth *d* is a kind of *t*)—the Proto-Indo-European form was likely *septm̥*. But not in Germanic, where you get things like German's *sieben*, Dutch's *zeven*, Danish's *syv*. Why? Well, Semitic languages have a *seven* word that sounds rather like Indo-European's but lacks that *t*: Biblical Hebrew's, for instance, was *šébaʕ*. Again, the *b* sound was a blowing, close to the *v* in *seven*, or the *f* in the Old English form *seofon*. And in Old High German, it came out as a straight *b* (*sibun*).

Phinding the Phoenicians

Okay—maybe. But what we want now is evidence that speakers of a Semitic language from way down in the Middle East actually migrated to the northern shore of Europe, namely, what is now Denmark and the northern tip of Germany, or the southern tips of Sweden and Norway right nearby. Here, the evidence helps us only so much.

We can know which Semitic speakers are of interest: it would be the Phoenicians, whose homeland was in today's Lebanon, Syria, and Israel. Their language, now extinct, was especially similar to Hebrew. The Phoenicians were one of those peoples of ancient history who were seized with a desire to travel and colonize, and they did so with great diligence on both the northern and southern shores of the Mediterranean, taking advantage of their advanced sailing technology. This included major colonies in North Africa, at Carthage, as well as one as far west as Spain, in what is now called Cádiz.

The Phoenicians even rounded the bend northward up into Portugal a tad . . . but there, the record stops. Did they sail up past the British Isles and round past the Netherlands to hit the neck of land shared today by Denmark and Germany?

There is no record that they did so. Apparently they were very secretive about their ship routes. Also, many of the northern European coastal regions they would have occupied have since sunk under the sea. This leaves us having to make nimble surmises.

The time, at least, was right. The Phoenicians had reached Portugal by the seventh century B.C., and were vanquished by the Romans by about 200 B.C. This would mean that if they reached Northern Europe, it would have been around the middle of the final millennium B.C.—when we know Proto-Germanic was in place. We do know that technology of the time allowed people to travel from the Mediterranean all the way around to that Danish-German necklet of land, because a Greek named Pytheas recorded having done exactly that in the late fourth century B.C. We do know that the Phoenicians' technology was up to the voyage, because the Vikings later sailed from

Northern Europe down to Britain and France in ships much less sturdy. Then, remember that so many of the orphan Proto-Germanic words are about sailing . . . and fish.

The hints get ever more tantalizing. What's up, for example, with the passing references to two gods, Phol and Balder, in a magic spell written in an ancient German ancestor, Old High German? The Phoenicians' god of gods was Baal. About which we note three things.

First, as it happens, when Proto-Germanic's sounds went weird, words that came into the language starting with *b* ended up starting with *p* instead. So, from Baal—if you can think where I'm going, "Paal," anyone?

Second, one thing that happened to sounds after that, when Proto-Germanic turned into Old High German, was that *p* became a *pf* sound, written as *ph*. Not that I want to give it away, but, ahem: not Paal but *Phaal*.

Finally, another thing about sounds in Proto-Germanic was that what came in from Proto-Indo-European as a long *a* (*aa*, written *ā*) ended up as a long *o* (*ō*). So *Phaal* became *Phool*.

Put all of that together, and if you wondered what the earlier form of a word *Phol* in Old High German was, then even if you had no intention of drawing a connection to Phoenician or anything else, you would trace it backward to—*Baal*, with a long *a* sound.

And then, the Phoenicians were also given to referring

to Baal as *Baal 'Addīr* ("God great")—that is, Great God. Sometimes they would write it as one word, *Baliddir,* or even a shorter version, *Baldir.* And there in that Old High German document is a god called *Balder.*

Finally, get this: not long ago, an intrepid German renegade archaeologist trawling the shallows of the North Sea found artifacts from between 1500 and 500 B.C. They were from, for one, Ancient Greece and the Minoan civilization of Crete, and then there were also remains of a Phoenician cooking pot! These findings were on the shore of Germany's northerly Schleswig-Holstein province: precisely one of the areas where Proto-Germanic is thought to have arisen.

Theo Vennemann of the University of Munich puts it that in light of all of the various indications pointing in one direction, "it would be amazing if the Phoenicians had excluded Germania from their frame of reference." In modern times, Vennemann has been the proponent par excellence of the hypothesis that Phoenician reshaped Proto-Germanic. All of the evidence in the previous paragraphs, as well as most of the Semitic-Germanic etymologies I have presented, is his work,[2] and I cotton to the

---

2. Vennemann also called my attention to the article in *Der Spiegel* reporting the discovery of the artifacts in Schleswig-Holstein.

I have not included Vennemann's argument that the reason Germanic languages (except English) keep the verb up front in second place because early Semitic languages put their verbs first, such that Phoenicians would have preferred keeping verbs as close to the beginning of sentences as possible in ren-

lawyerly kind of argumentation from fragmentary evidence that he excels at.

However, unlike in the other chapters, this will not be the place where I muse as to why linguists have not accepted Vennemann's case hands down. Part of why his work is not mentioned in traditional sources is that most of it is published in obscure venues and often in German, while the main other source on the subject argues for influence from Semitic on Germanic only within a larger case for Semitic's impact on Indo-European as a whole, in two magnum opuses so majestically magnum as to ward off all but super-specialists and obsessives.

However, the truth is that even if the Phoenician case had been presented in Anglophone reader-friendly articles in prominent journals, it would stand as a mere intriguing possibility until there are etymologies of a good several dozen of the orphan Proto-Germanic

---

dering Proto-Germanic. Although the argument is interesting, my intent has been to maintain a focus on what made for Modern English, and Modern English lacks the V2 rule (although Old English had it).

Similarly, Vennemann is devoted not only to the Phoenician argument, but to one stipulating that Proto-Germanic vocabulary and accent patterns were affected by relatives of Basque once spoken across Europe before Proto-Indo-European spread across the continent and marginalized Basque. (Today, Basque is spoken in a small region straddling France and Spain and has no living relatives.) Vennemann's work in this vein is also admirable, but I have not included it because it applies to other Indo-European language families as well, including Celtic and the Romance languages. For the sake of keeping the throughline as focused as possible, I have restricted this book to issues unique to English.

Vennemann puts forth both of these arguments in "Zur Entstehung des Germanischen," *Sprachwissenschaft* 25 (2000): 233–69.

words. At this point, there are only about fifteen Semitic etymologies, and many of them are not of orphan words, but proposed as alternative etymologies for words long considered ordinary descendants from Proto-Indo-European.

More archaeological evidence would also help. That scholars have so far not been even looking for such evidence means that the effort may be fruitful, but it must be put forth. Moreover, scholars uninterested short of detailed historical documentation of how many Phoenicians settled exactly where, and whether or not they picked up Proto-Germanic and passed their rendition down to future generations, would be unclear on the scripture versus writing issue we have seen in this book: in 500 B.C. no Phoenician could have conceived of committing such mundane observations into writing. The linguistic data would have to be allowed to clinch the case, as with the Celtic and Viking impacts on English.

However, in those cases, we at least know that the relevant people were in England at the right time. One broken pot cannot make the case for the Phoenicians, especially since Phoenician goods could easily have been carried to Northern Europe amid trade, without the Phoenicians themselves traveling with them, much less settling there for good and transforming the local language forever.

Yet I cannot resist tossing in one more thing pointing

in a certain direction. One of the Phoenicians' main colonies was at Carthage in North Africa. Carthaginians were champion travelers; as much Phoenician migration started there as from today's Middle East. In the Phoenician dialect spoken in Carthage, Punic words could not begin with *p*. The words that began with *p* in earlier Phoenician had come in Punic to begin with—three guesses—*f*. Fopcorn in Tunisia!

What Proto-Germanic Was, What English Is

Unsettled though it currently is, the Phoenician case is worth ending this book with. First, I think the evidence is suggestive enough that it demands wider airing than it has gotten thus far. Second, however, even if there never emerges enough evidence to support the specific idea that Proto-Germanic was Proto-Indo-European as rendered by Phoenician adults, the sheer difference between Germanic and other branches of Indo-European makes a strong case that Proto-Germanic, before it split into today's Germanic languages, was already a language deeply affected by adults of some extraction learning it as a second language. "Fopcorn." *Sleep, slept, write, wrote.* Every second case and tense marker from its ancestral language lost to the wind. Every third word unknown in the language that gave birth to it.

The lesson: the idea that there was once an English

somehow pristine, a pure issuance, is false. Even the Proto-Germanic language that gave birth to Old English was one that had seemed, to those who spoke its own Proto-Indo-European ancestor, perverted by speakers of something else.

Long before Old English started taking on words from Old Norse and then French and Latin, in a fashion that we today read as so cosmopolitan, Proto-Germanic had taken on countless words from some other language. Yet the isolated, parochial tribespeople who spoke it were not cosmopolitan in the least. They knew and cared little of the world beyond them except as a prospect for land and plunder. They were not hoarding new words as part of building a mighty literature, as they were illiterate. They took on new words because there were new people among them who used those words—as humans have done worldwide since the dawn of our species, and as Old English speakers did—passively, unremarkably. The diversity of the English vocabulary is something we should celebrate as evidence of Anglophones' universal humanity, not as a feather in our cultural cap.

Meanwhile, Old English's grammar was not, in any logical sense, an untainted system later ill-used by lazy moderns. It was the product of the distortion of Proto-Indo-European by adults ill-equipped to master it fully. People today bemoan the eclipse of *whom*'s marking of the accusative, unaware that Proto-Germanic speakers let go four of the cases that Proto-Indo-European speakers used. The world kept turning. You don't like *nucular*? Well, how do you think the likes of "fopcorn" sounded to a Proto-Germanic speaker watching that kind of pronunciation spread? Yet we today have no interest in undoing the "damage" and saying "pah-ther" instead of "father."

For all of the pleasures of contemplating photographs of ancient manuscripts, reading about *shirt* versus *skirt* and *pig* versus *pork*, savoring strophes of Chaucer and reminding ourselves how good Shakespeare was, The History of English we are usually given is rather static. Some marauders brought Old English to Britain. The Celts scampered away. Pretty soon the Brits went cosmopolitan and started gathering baskets of words from assorted folks, such that now we have a bigger vocabulary than before. The only thing that happened to English grammar during all this time, other than minutiae only a linguist could love, is that it lost a lot of endings, and this made word order less flexible.

The History of English is more than that. An offshoot of Proto-Indo-European borrowed a third of its vocabulary from another language. That language may have been Phoenician; certainly, there was some language. Its speakers submitted the Proto-Indo-European offshoot to a grammatical overhaul. As adults, they could not help shaving off a lot of its complications, and rendering parts of the grammar in ways familiar to them from their native language. This left Proto-Germanic a language both mixed and abbreviated before it even gave birth to new languages—and meant that it passed this mixed, abbreviated nature on to those new languages.

One of them was Old English, which morphed merrily along carrying the odd sound patterns, vowel-switching past marking, and mystery vocabulary from Proto-Germanic, just as organisms morph along through the ages carrying and replicating mitochondrial DNA patterns tracing back to the dawn of life. Old English was taken up by speakers of yet another language—or in this case, languages: Celtic ones. As Celts started using English more and more over the decades, English gradually took an infusion of grammatical features from Welsh and Cornish, including a usage of *do* known in no other languages on earth.

Not long afterward, speakers of yet one more language filtered English yet again. Vikings speaking Old Norse picked up the language fast, and gave it a second shave, so to speak, after what had happened to Proto-Germanic over on the Continent more than a thousand years beforehand. English's grammar became the least "fussy" of all of the Germanic languages, impatient with "nuance" as Edward Sapir had it, and leaving its speakers, like Mark

Twain, with a special challenge in mastering the complexities of other Germanic languages.

The result: a tongue oddly genderless and telegraphic for a European one, clotted with peculiar ways of using *do* and progressive *-ing*—with, in addition, indeed, a great big bunch of words from other languages. Not only Norse, French, Latin, and Greek, but possibly Phoenician—or if not, some other language, but surely that.

The vanilla version of The History of English will live on. But its proponents have not had occasion to engage with the underground stories I have attempted to share with you, or, having done so briefly, have opted to sweep them under the rug in favor of continuing in their accustomed *grooves*, to adopt the terminology of the Whorfian cited in the previous chapter.

Understandable. But the actual History of English is not only more scientifically plausible, but also more *interesting*—worthy of engagement, retention, and further study—than the traditional one all about the supposedly miraculous fact that people who invaded England left a lot of their words behind. Who has ever been truly moved by that?

To bring the book full circle by quoting the Introduction, English is miscegenated, abbreviated. *Interesting.*

Notes on Sources

Introduction

The translations of the oh-so-spontaneous sentence rendered in German, Dutch, and Norwegian were confirmed for me by Sean Boggs, Peter Bakker, and Kurt Rice, respectively.

One

WE SPEAK A MISCEGENATED GRAMMAR

Welsh *do*: Gareth King, *Modern Welsh: A Comprehensive Grammar* (London: Routledge, 2003), p. 189.

Welsh progressive: Ingo Mittendorf and Erich Poppe, "Celtic Contacts of the English Progressive?" in *The Celtic Englishes II*, ed. by Hildegard L. C. Tristram (Heidelberg: C. Winter, 2000), p. 118.

Cornish *do*: Henry Jenner, *A Handbook of the Cornish Language* (London: David Nutt, 1904), pp. 116–17.

Cornish progressive: Mittendorf and Poppe, p. 118.

Bryson quote: Bill Bryson, *The Mother Tongue: English and How It Got That Way* (New York: William Morrow & Co., 1990), p. 49.

Genetic data on England: Stephen Oppenheimer, *The Origins of the British: A Genetic Detective Story* (New York: Carroll & Graf, 2006), pp. 379, 412–13.

Burial styles: Heinrich Härke, "Population Replacement or Acculturation? An Archaeological Perspective on Population and Migration in Post-Roman Britain," in *The Celtic Englishes III*, ed. by Hildegard L. C. Tristram (Heidelberg: C. Winter, 2003), p. 19.

King Ine's laws: Referred to in Härke, consulted in John M. Stearns, *The Germs and Developments of the Laws of England Embracing the Anglo-Saxon Laws* (New York: Banks & Brothers, 1889). (Kessinger Publishing reprint)

Crystal quote: David Crystal, *The Cambridge Encyclopedia of the English Language* (Cambridge: Cambridge University Press, 1995), p. 8.

Jamaican patois sentence: Robert LePage and David DeCamp, *Jamaican Creole* (London: MacMillan, 1960).

Twi sentence: Rev. J. G. Christaller, *A Grammar of the Asante and Fante Languages Called Tshi.* (Basel: Basel Evangelical Missionary Society, 1875), p. 118.

Germanic *do*: Unfortunately the most thorough examination and the closest one to being handy is in German: Werner Abraham and C. Jac Conradie, *Präteritumschwund und Diskursgrammatik* (Amsterdam: John Benjamins, 2001), pp. 83, 87.

Nanai sentence: V. A. Arvorin, *Sintaksicheshie Issledovania po Nanaiskomu Jazyku* (Leningrad: Nauka, 1981), pp. 79–80.

Italian *do*-support: Paola Beninca and Cecilia Poletto, "A Case of *Do*-support in Romance," *Natural Language and Linguistic Theory* 22 (2004): 51–94.

"Regularity" account of meaningless *do*: Andrew Garrett, "On the Origin of Auxiliary *Do*," *English Language and Linguistics* 2 (1998): 283–330.

Meaningless *do* and verb placement: Tony Kroch, John Myhill, and Susan Pintzuk, "Understanding *Do*," *Papers from the Chicago Linguistics Symposium* 18 (1982): 282–94.

Old High German sentence: Erich Poppe, "Progress on the Progressive? A Report," in *The Celtic Englishes III*, ed. by Hildegard L. C. Tristram (Heidelberg: C. Winter, 2003), p. 71.

Colloquial Indonesian versus written Indonesian: David Gil, "Escaping Eurocentrism: Fieldwork as a Process of

Unlearning," in *Linguistic Fieldwork*, ed. by Paul Newman and Martha Ratliff (Cambridge: Cambridge University Press, 2001).

Dante and Italian: Daniel J. Boorstin, *The Creators* (New York: Vintage, 1992), pp. 258–59.

Arabic dialects: Alan Kaye and Judith Rosenhouse, "Arabic Dialects and Maltese," in *The Semitic Languages*, ed. by Robert Hetzron (London: Routledge, 1997), p. 309.

Spanish in Ecuador: John Lipski, *Latin American Spanish* (London: Longman, 1994), p. 251.

Old English speakers' culinary options: Robert Lacey and Danny Danziger, *The Year 1000* (Boston: Little, Brown & Co, 1999), pp. 136–38.

Uralic and Russian: Valentin Kiparsky, *Gibt es ein Finno-ugrisches Substrat im Slavischen?* (Helsinki: Suomalainen Tiedeakatemia, 1969), p. 23.

Dravidian and Indo-Aryan: Thomas Burrow, *The Sanskrit Language* (London: Faber & Faber, 1955), pp. 380–86.

Possible Celtic loanwords: Andrew Breeze, "Seven Types of Celtic Loanword," in *The Celtic Roots of English*, ed. by Markku Filppula, Juhani Klemola, and Heli Pitkänen (Joensuu, Finland: University of Joensuu Faculty of Humanities, 2002), pp. 175–81.

Northern Subject Rule: Juhani Klemola, "The Origins of the Northern Subject Rule: A Case of Early Contact?" in

The Celtic Englishes II, ed. by Hildegard L. C. Tristram (Heidelberg: C. Winter, 2000), p. 337.

Passage from traditional judgment of Celtic contribution: Tauno F. Mustanoja, *A Middle English Syntax, Part I* (*Parts of Speech*) (Helsinki: Société Néophilologique, 1960), pp. 584–89.

Going to history: Culled from an especially accessible account, Guy Deutscher, *The Unfolding of Language* (New York: Metropolitan, 2005), pp. 146–51.

Dalby: Andrew Dalby, *Dictionary of Languages* (New York: Columbia University Press, 1998), p. 675.

McCrum et al. quote: Robert McCrum, William Cran, and Robert MacNeil, *The Story of English* (New York: Viking, 1986), p. 61.

Crystal quote: David Crystal, *The Cambridge Encyclopedia of the English Language* (Cambridge: Cambridge University Press, 1995), p.8.

Two

A LESSON FROM THE CELTIC IMPACT

Cantonese data: Stephen Matthews and Virginia Yip, *Cantonese: A Comprehensive Grammar* (London: Routledge, 1994), p. 56.

Frisian data: Pieter Tiersma, *Frisian Reference Grammar* (Dordrecht: Foris, 1985), pp. 55–56, 77, 116.

Nineteenth-century "errors": Richard W. Bailey, *Nineteenth-*

Century English (Ann Arbor: University of Michigan Press, 1996), pp. 215–61.

Portuguese-English book: Pedro Carolino, *The New Guide of the Conversation in Portuguese and English* (Boston: James R. Osgood & Co., 1883), p. 120. (This source is usually encountered today in abridged editions; I refer to an ancient copy of the entire book.)

Three
WE SPEAK A BATTERED GRAMMAR

Old English and Old Norse sentences: Robert Lacey and Danny Danziger, *The Year 1000* (Boston: Little, Brown & Co, 1999), pp. 33–34.

Sapir quote: Edward Sapir, *Language: An Introduction to the Study of Speech* (New York: Harcourt Brace, 1921), pp. 169–70.

Number of Normans: John Gillingham, "The Early Middle Ages," in *The Oxford History of Britain*, ed. by Kenneth O. Morgan (Oxford: Oxford University Press, 1988), p. 121.

William of Nassyngton: David Crystal, *The Cambridge Encyclopedia of the English Language* (Cambridge: Cambridge University Press, 1995), p. 31.

Linguistic equilibrium: R. M. W. Dixon, *The Rise and Fall of Languages* (Cambridge: Cambridge University Press, 1997).

Welsh case markers and Old English: An example is Hildegard L. C. Tristram, "Attrition of Inflections in English and Welsh," in *The Celtic Roots of English*, ed. by Markku Filppula, Juhani Klemola, and Heli Pitkänen, (Joensuu, Finland: University of Joensuu Faculty of Humanities, 2002), pp. 111–49.

Altaic-Mandarin hybrid languages: Examples most handy are three consecutive articles on the Hezhou, Tangwang, and Wutun dialects, on pp. 865–97 in a volume commonly available in university libraries: *Atlas of Languages of Intercultural Communication in the Pacific, Asia, and the Americas* (Volume II.2), ed. by Stephen A. Wurm, Peter Mühlhäusler, and Darrell T. Tryon (Berlin: Mouton de Gruyter, 1996).

Concentration of Danes: John Blair, "The Anglo-Saxon Period," in *The Oxford History of Britain*, ed. by Kenneth O. Morgan (Oxford: Oxford University Press, 1988), pp. 107–8.

Northern English suffixes: Sarah Grey Thomason and Terence Kaufman, *Language Contact, Creolization, and Genetic Linguistics* (Berkeley: University of California Press, 1988), p. 278.

Dorset gender: William Barnes, *A Glossary of the Dorset Dialect with a Grammar of Its Word Shapening and Wording* (London: Trübner & Co., 1886), p. 17–18.

Case markers in Gamalson inscription: Tamas Eitler, "An Old Norse–Old English Contact Phenomenon: The Retention of the Dative Plural Inflection -um in the Northumbrian Dialect of Old English, in *The Even Yearbook* 5, ed. by Laszlo Varga (Budapest: Eotvos Lorand University Department of English Linguistics Working Papers, 2002), pp. 31–48.

"You mistake you" observation: Kirsti Peitsara, "The Development of Reflexive Strategies in English," in *Grammaticalization at Work*, ed. by Matti Rissanen, Merja Kytö, and Kirsi Heikkonen (Berlin: Mouton de Gruyter, 1997), p. 337.

Matti Rissanen, "Whatever Happened to the Middle English Indefinite Pronouns?" in *Studies in Middle English Linguistics*, ed. by Jacek Fisiak (Berlin: Mouton de Gruyter, 1997), pp. 513–29.

Favorite star: Roger Lass, "Phonology and Morphology," in *The Cambridge History of the English Language* (Vol. 2), ed. by Norman Blake (Cambridge: Cambridge University Press, 1992), pp. 23–155.

Schwa-drop observation: Thomason and Kaufman, p. 277.

Funny passage on gender in English: Chun-fat Lau, "Gender in the Hakka Dialect: Suffixes with Gender in

More Than 40 Nouns," *Journal of Chinese Linguistics* 27 (1999): 124–31.

Hashimoto on Chinese: Mantaro Hashimoto, "The Alta-icization of Northern Chinese," in *Contributions to Sino-Tibetan Studies*, ed. by John McCoy and Timothy Light (Leiden: E. J. Brill, 1986), pp. 76–97.

Four

DOES OUR GRAMMAR CHANNEL OUR THOUGHT?

Standard go-to Whorf text: John B. Carroll, ed., *Language, Thought, and Reality: Selected Writings of Benjamin Lee Whorf* (Cambridge, MA: MIT Press, 1956).

Kawesqar: Jack Hitt, "Say No More," *The New York Times*, February 29, 2004.

"Users of markedly . . .": Carroll, p. 221.

"Newtonian space . . .": Carroll, p. 153.

Hopi data: Ekkehart Malotki, *Hopi Time: A Linguistic Analysis of the Temporal Concepts in the Hopi Language* (Berlin: Mouton de Gruyter, 1983), p. 534.

"No words . . .": Carroll, p. 57.

"Potential range . . .": Carroll, p. 117.

"We cut nature up . . .": Carroll, pp. 213–14.

"It might be said . . .": Carroll, p. 151.

"The thought of the individual . . .": Dorothy Lee,

"Conceptual Implications of an Indian Language," *Philosophy of Science* 5 (1938): 89–102.

"It is clear that linguistic determinism . . .": Carroll, p. 117.

Clark: Herbert H. Clark, "Communities, Commonalities, and Communication," in *Rethinking Linguistic Relativity*, ed. by John J. Gumperz and Stephen C. Levinson (Cambridge: Cambridge University Press, 1996), p. 343.

Wilson on Russian: Lewis A. Dabney, *Edmund Wilson: A Life in Literature* (New York: Farrar, Straus & Giroux, 2005), p. 409.

French verbs: Mark Abley, *Spoken Here: Travels Among Threatened Languages* (Boston: Houghton Mifflin, 2003), p. 48.

Boro verbs: Abley, pp. 122–27.

Second in European languages: Martin Haspelmath, "The European Linguistic Area: Standard Average European," in *Language Typology and Language Universals: An International Handbook*, ed. by Martin Haspelmath, Ekkehard König, Wulf Österreicher, and Wolfgang Raible (Berlin: Mouton de Gruyter, 2001), pp. 1495, 1503.

"Does the Hopi . . .": Carroll, p. 85.

"Our objectified view . . .": Carroll, p. 153.

Montagnais: Abley, pp. 276–77.

Cree: Thomas Payne, *Describing Morphosyntax: A Guide for*

Field Linguists (Cambridge: Cambridge University Press, 1997), p. 211.

Hypothetical Chinese sentence: Charles N. Li and Sandra A. Thompson, *Mandarin Chinese: A Functional Reference Grammar* (Berkeley: University of California Press, 1981), p. 647.

Bloom study: Aldred H. Bloom, *The Linguistic Shaping of Thought: A Study in the Impact of Language on Thinking in China and the West* (Hillsdale, NJ: Lawrence Erlbaum, 1981).

Sign language: Leah Hager Cohen, "Deafness as Metaphor, Not Gimmick," *The New York Times*, August 23, 2003.

Guugu Yimithirr: Stephen C. Levinson, "Relativity in Spatial Conception and Description," in *Rethinking Linguistic Relativity*, ed. by John J. Gumperz and Stephen C. Levinson (Cambridge: Cambridge University Press, 1996), pp. 180–81.

Pirahã: Dan Everett, "Cultural Constraints on Grammar and Cognition in Pirahã: Another Look at the Design Features of Human Language," *Current Anthropology* 46: 621–46.

Everett on language as thought: He told me, on April 13, 2007.

Gender and thought: Lera Boroditsky, Lauren A. Schmidt, and Webb Phillips, "Sex, Syntax, and Semantics," in *Lan-*

guage in Mind: Advances in the Study of Language and Thought, ed. by Dedre Gentner and Susan Goldin-Meadow (Cambridge: MIT Press, 2003), pp. 79–91.

Imagining gendered voices: M. Sera, C. Berge, and J. del Castillo, "Grammatical and Conceptual Forces in the Attribution of Gender by English and Spanish Speakers," *Cognitive Development* 9: 261–92.

Kay quote: Paul Kay, "Intra-Speaker Relativity," in *Rethinking Linguistic Relativity*, ed. by John J. Gumperz and Stephen C. Levinson (Cambridge: Cambridge University Press, 1996), p. 110.

Paul Kay and Willett Kempton, "What Is the Sapir-Whorf Hypothesis?" *American Anthropologist* 86 (1984): 66.

Barnard and Spencer: Alan Barnard and Jonathan Spencer, eds., *Encyclopedia of Social and Cultural Anthropology* (London: Routledge, 1996).

Textbook: Conrad Phillip Kottak, *Cultural Anthropology* (New York: McGraw Hill, 2002).

Five

SKELETONS IN THE CLOSET

Statement on orphan words: Don Ringe, *From Proto-Indo-European to Proto-Germanic* (New York: Oxford University Press, 2006), pp. 295–96.

Semitic etymologies of *fright*, *folk*, and *maiden*: Theo Vennemann has presented these in many places; the handiest is in German ("Zur Entstehung des Germanischen," *Sprachwissenschaft* 25 [2000]: 233–69). However, the most accessible English-language source is Vennemann's website, which includes a handout outline of a comprehensive presentation Vennemann has given on the topic.

Historical evidence for Phoenicians' travel northward: The handiest source in English is Theo Vennemann, "*Phol, Balder,* and the Birth of Germanic," in *Etymologie, Entlehnungen und Entwicklungen: Festschrift für Jorma Koivulehto zum 70. Geburtstag,* ed. by Irma Hyvärinen, Petri Kallo, and Jarmo Korhonen (Helsinki: Mémoire de la Société de Néophilologie de Helsinki LXIII, 2004), pp. 439–57; see also Vennemann's website.

Hebrew *cross* and *shore* and Old English *ofer*: Saul Levin, *Semitic and Indo-European: The Principal Etymologies, with Observations on Afro-Asiatic* (Amsterdam: John Benjamins, 1995), pp. 367–75.

Semitic source for Germanic *seven*: Levin, pp. 409–12.

Magnum opuses: Saul Levin, *The Indo-European and Semitic Languages* (Albany: State University of New York Press, 1971); Saul Levin, *Semitic and Indo-European: The Principal Etymologies, with Observations on Afro-Asiatic* (Amsterdam: John Benjamins, 1995).

Artifacts in North Sea: Matthias Schulz, "Göttertränen im Watt," *Der Spiegel* (December 4, 2006): 160–62.

Acknowledgments

This book is based on detours in my academic research. My primary research focus has been on creole languages, but certain strains of my arguments in that realm have led me, by chance, to investigations of why English is the deeply peculiar language that it is, compared to its closest relatives, the other languages in the Germanic family.

Over time I realized that this research, taken together, constituted a revised conception of what English is and why. I found emerging in me a certain irresistible desire now familiar as the spark for all of my books: to get what was sticking in my craw down in book form.

I sensed that the point of the book would not lend itself to the process via which books are presented to agents and publishers: summarizing the ideas in outline form. I predicted that in bullet-point format, the thrust of the book would seem too in-house, too pointy-headed, too specialized.

So I did an end run and just wrote the book unbidden and submitted a whole draft to my agent. Much to my surprise, she, Katinka Matson, loved it, and to my further surprise, my now regular publisher, Gotham Books, did, too.

As such, my first acknowledgment is to Katinka, and to William Shinker at Gotham, for being open to a book with such a weird focus. Thanks also to Patrick Mulligan at Gotham for making the manuscript better—and notably for coming up with "Volcanoes" as the mnemonic for Icelandic.

I am also grateful to linguists Werner Abraham, Östen Dahl, Andrew Garrett, Gary Holland, Fred Karlsson, John Payne, Irmengard Rauch, Elizabeth Traugott, Theo Vennemann, and David White for their support for and feedback on the articles that this book is based on. Special thanks to Elly Van Gelderen, a sterling researcher on the history of English but open to new ideas, for first tipping me off that the folks arguing that English is shot through with Celtic influence are not crazy.

My argumentation was also sharpened by feedback at presentations of my work at the University of California, Berkeley, the University of Helsinki, the University of

Tromsø, the University of Toronto, and the University of Manchester.

Finally, my wife, Martha, read all of the chapters in first draft and restrained me from something linguists writing for the general public must guard against, a tendency to luxuriate in idle details under the impression that this will be comfort food to the general reader. Thank you, Martha, for "getting it" as you do because you have spent years listening to me gabbing about language and linguistics, but remaining aware of how my presentation will come off to readers who did not happen to marry me.

Index